The Nature and Character of GOD

All titles in the series
Good News in John 3:16

All titles available as paperback, hardcover, e-book, audiobook and video. See Rushwave.org

The Nature and Character of God

The Judgment God Desires to Withhold

The Blessing God Desires to Bestow

The Eternal Son of God

The Saving Work of Jesus Christ

The Faith God Requires to Save

The Nature and Character of GOD

Understanding the One who has no beginning and no end

Bert Davidson

RUSHWAVE®
Litchfield, Illinois. United States
rushwave.org

The Nature and Character of God
Copyright © 2020 Bert Davidson
Author website: bertdavidson.com

All rights reserved. No part of this book may be used or reproduced in any manner whatsoever without written permission, except in the case of brief quotations in critical articles and reviews. See rushwave.org permissions page.

Published by Rushwave®
Litchfield, Illinois. United States
Publisher website: rushwave.org
Rushwave® and the Rushwave logo ® are registered trademarks

Published 2020. Version 11.26.22

This book is available in multiple formats. See rushwave.org
ISBN 978-1-62179-001-3 (paperback)
ISBN 978-1-62179-002-0 (hardcover)
ISBN 978-1-62179-003-7 (e-book–EPUB)
ISBN 978-1-62179-004-4 (audio book)
ISBN 978-1-62179-014-3 (video)

Scripture quotations taken from the New American Standard Bible® (NASB). Copyright © 1960, 1962, 1963, 1968, 1971, 1972, 1973, 1975, 1977, 1995 by The Lockman Foundation.
Used by permission. www.Lockman.org

Library of Congress Control Number: 2022950424

Contents

1. Good News in John 3:16 11
2. How your God Impacts Everyday Life 14
3. What do you mean by "God"? 20
4. There is One God 23
5. God Created and Sustains All Things 28
6. God has no Form 37
7. God is Always There 41
8. God is Eternal 46
9. God is All-Knowing 49
10. God is All-Wise 57
11. God is All-Powerful 64
12. God is Just and Righteous 71
13. God Abounds in Truth 76
14. God has Emotions and Feelings 80
15. God can be Pleased 83
16. God can be Grieved 88
17. God can be Provoked 93
18. God is Love 100
19. "God" as used in John 3:16 106

    Suggested Reading *109*

Visit Rushwave.org...112

The Nature and Character of God

For **God** *so loved the world,
that He gave His only begotten Son,
that whoever believes in Him
shall not perish, but have eternal life.*

John 3:16

Chapter 1

Good News in John 3:16

One sentence relates six core teachings which detail the worldview of Jesus Christ.

From God's perspective mankind is broken, lost, and headed for destruction. But it is to this fallen, corrupt, chaotic world that God has good news. This good news relates the worldview and core teachings of one Person, Jesus Christ, as encapsulated in a single, profound statement from the historical record of His life. Whether Jesus Himself made the statement, or whether it was a comment supplied by the writer who spent years with Jesus, is unimportant. Either way, it concisely expresses the solemn truths Jesus Himself taught. The statement is found in the Bible, the book of John, chapter three, verse sixteen.

> *For God so loved the world, that He gave His only begotten Son, that whoever believes in Him shall not perish, but have eternal life.* JOHN 3:16

Every word in this sentence has a deep, clear meaning, and there is a specific way Jesus would have us understand "God," "gave," "Son," "believes," "perish," and "eternal life." While understanding the meaning of these words does not in any way require a higher education, we must be careful not to project *our own meaning* onto each word so as to align with *our own worldview*. There is no shortage of people who take the words of Jesus and project onto them meanings which are completely foreign to anything He ever taught.

To guard against this error of misinterpreting Jesus' words, we must consult the body of work which references His life and teachings: the Bible. In doing so, we will not only be consulting the record of Jesus' own words, but also of those whom He directly called, taught and commissioned (men called "apostles"), as well as those historical figures whom He regarded as God's spokesmen (men called "prophets").

The good news of John 3:16 can be broken down into six parts, and each addresses a different and very profound subject. This book series is comprised of six books which correspond to each subject.

Book 1 addresses THE NATURE AND CHARACTER OF GOD, for it is impossible to properly interpret the statement "For *God* so loved the world" without clearly outlining what the word "God" means. In this book God's attributes are described in a way that clearly differentiates Him from other gods that have been worshiped and suggested throughout history.

Book 2, THE JUDGMENT GOD DESIRES TO WITHHOLD, has the word "perish" in focus: "For God so loved the world ... that whoever believes in Him shall not *perish*." We shall see that perishing involves punishment and suffering in a life after death — a punishment God Himself is obligated in justice to impose, but which He nonetheless desires to spare man from.

Book three, THE BLESSING GOD DESIRES TO BESTOW, shifts focus from what God wants to save us from to what He desires to bless us with: eternal life. "For God so loved the world, that ... whoever believes in Him shall ... have *eternal life*." And we shall see there is much more involved in eternal life then mere immortality.

Book four addresses THE ETERNAL SON OF GOD, Jesus Christ, and the many different truths concerning Himself in relation to God and man. "For God so loved the world, that He gave *His only begotten Son*." Understanding the Person of Jesus Christ is vital to understanding God Himself and His love for the world.

Book five, THE SAVING WORK OF JESUS CHRIST, corresponds to the words "God so *loved the world, that He gave* His only begotten Son." We will consider the purpose, meaning, and implications of the death of Jesus Christ.

Finally, book six reveals THE FAITH GOD REQUIRES TO SAVE, and we shall see it is trusting in the only begotten Son of God, Jesus Christ. "For God so loved the world, that He gave His only begotten Son, that *whoever believes in Him* shall not perish." Contrary to what many think, God is not going to grant eternal life to everyone. There is a condition that must be met.

> **It may seem hard to believe, but it is nonetheless true: John 3:16 is a worldview that can bring your entire life into perspective. To understand each word in this sentence as Jesus meant it to be understood; to contemplate the entire message; to allow its truth to penetrate your heart and enlighten your mind — this results in an understanding that far exceeds anything you can imagine. And it is just one sentence: "For God so loved the world, that He gave His only begotten Son, that whoever believes in Him shall not perish, but have eternal life." JOHN 3:16**

Chapter 2

How your God Impacts Everyday Life

Your conception of God is merely one of many in the history of the world, and it affects everything.

Over much of human history societies believed in multiple gods as mystically present in idols. A choice stone would be selected or a suitable tree cut down, and it would be carved into the image of the god — a figure of a man with a muscular physique, a woman with multiple limbs, or a human like figure with the head of a bird and the body of a man. The object would be skillfully crafted and beautifully adorned, perhaps even overlaid with gold, silver, or other precious things. The various idols would then be worshiped as a god.

Idols were often very large, but even in those cases similar idols would be made of the pocket-size variety so they could be placed in the home or taken along while traveling. In this way protection and blessing could be provided by the idols.

The idols in each culture represented a worldview that affected all aspects of everyday life. It would be a serious mistake to deem these idols in different cultures as merely different conceptions of the form the gods took. The image was representative of an entire belief system. One culture may have an idol with the head of a bird and the body of a man, while another culture may have an idol that is entirely an animal. Both cultures worshiped their idols and viewed their gods as being present in the idol in some mystical way. But the conception of the gods as embodied in the idols was not only different in appearance, but also in the nature and character of the gods, the relationship of the gods to man, and numerous aspects of life.

So what parts of everyday life did these conceptions of god affect? The answer is everything, and modern day and ancient religions provide numerous examples.

The gods in these various belief systems differed in their nature and character. They could be viewed as capable of warring with each other, pro-creating, acting impurely towards one another, engaging in deception, displaying fits of temper, or even being tricked themselves.

These gods differed in the powers they possessed. Different gods could control the weather, determine the outcome of wars, make a barren woman conceive, ensure a bountiful crop, bring diseases on one's enemies, and effect or prevent natural catastrophes such as earthquakes or volcanic eruptions.

The gods determined those rituals and worship practices by which they were appeased and their blessings secured. There was an entire spectrum of activity here depending on the god a culture served: human sacrifices, animal sacrifices, afflicting or cutting one-self, building of sanctuaries, or participation in festivals with specific religious rites and elaborate costumes and dances. If you were a hunter, you would appeal to the hunting god to secure favor in the hunt. If you were a farmer, you would perform those activities that pleased the rain god.

The Nature and Character of God

And if you were barren, you would seek to please the god of fertility to enable conception.

A person's god was involved in how to pray effectively. One culture would place certain ritual prayers on a small wheel that could be turned by the wind. Every time the wheel turned, it would be deemed as having the same positive effect as reciting a prayer and thereby secure a good outcome. Another culture would cut themselves with lances when appealing to the gods in an attempt to move them to action.

A person's god was involved in gaining wisdom for critical decisions. Gaining this wisdom could involve consulting people deemed to have various powers or connections: an astrologer to interpret the stars; a witch-doctor to call up the dead; a priest or priestess to receive an oracle from the gods; or a shaman who in a trance could travel through time and access good and evil spirits.

Moral standards of right and wrong involved the gods. In one culture, the ability to with a straight-face tell a lie and shortchange another person was deemed a virtuous trait worthy of imitation. Committing suicide by throwing oneself on the funeral pyre of a deceased husband was deemed an honorable act of self-sacrifice. And putting a disfigured infant to death was deemed a compassionate way to end their miserable life.

The gods played a role in what was acceptable sexually in society either by approving of certain sexual activity, being indifferent towards it, or in some cases requiring various forms of sexual expression to secure blessing. There was an entire spectrum of activity here, and what would be deemed either criminal or a social taboo in one culture would be met with indifference or even celebrated in another culture. There were cultures with marriage between one man and one woman, marriage between one man and several women, as well as casual unmarried sexual relationships between one man and one woman. There was also homosexuality, lesbianism, transsexualism, incest, bestiality, and other practices.

The gods played a role in how one's body was connected to the hereafter. A culture which believed in reincarnation may revolt at the idea of amputating a gangrenous limb; doing so would mean that person would come back in the next life without that limb. Better to not even consider amputation and die with that body part, than come back in the next life without it.

Concepts of the afterlife related to one's god, and even to burial practices. In one tribe burying a live infant along with a dying father would secure benefits for both the child and the father in the afterlife. Failure to conform to this practice would be deemed dishonoring of one's father and result in being ostracized from the tribe.

A person's god shaped their perspective on the sanctity of life. In some cultures the lame, disfigured, or mentally ill were deemed at worst cursed or at best useless. Better to just either let them die or put them to death rather than incur the wrath of the gods or burden society. In other cases entire people groups were considered disposable because they either did not possess what was deemed superior physical traits, or they came from a different family line.

People generally continued in their worldview day after day, year after year, in keeping with their upbringing and societal norms. Fathers would obtain the pocket idol to place in their home and protect the family. Mothers would ready the children to attend a religious festival where the highpoint was the witnessing of a human sacrifice. Yes, it made everyone squirm, but there was a part of them that wanted to see it. Every morning amulets would be donned to protect from evil spirits. Prayers would continue to be inscribed on wheels in hope the gods would hear. Husbands going off to war would visit the temple to pay homage to the gods that were half-man and half-animal in hope they would be protected in battle, and be able to return to their wives. And this continued on and on, day after day, year after year, with thousands of different tribes, people groups and civilizations rising and falling — many of which are now extinct, and others which continue to the present day.

Your conception of God affects all aspects of your life. Irrespective of whether you believe God has a specific form — you may not believe He is represented in a half-bird and half-man statue — you definitely have a *conception* of His nature and character: what pleases Him, what His thoughts are towards man, what makes Him angry, and what He deems right and wrong. You have views regarding what He deems are acceptable forms of worship: what religious rites are to be observed, how and when to pray, and what images or pictorial representations of Him are accurate. You also have other related beliefs surrounding your concept of God: what happens after you die, what relationship there is between your body and the hereafter, whether you are rewarded or punished by Him in this life and the next, and the basis on which He effects those rewards and punishments.

But your concept of God affects much more than just aspects of religious service. Your conception affects everyday, practical things also. How does your god prescribe overcoming an addictive, destructive habit? Or is there even a strategy He provides? What about dealing with sickness, pain and disease? Does He even want you to pray about such matters?

And if you do pray, will He answer? And if it depends, on what does it depend? What does your God say about human life? Is all life sacred, or are only those who are born "normal" worthy of protection and care? And what constitutes being born "normal"? And what about the intimate things of life such as sexuality. What is the view of your God on this matter? Is there *any* activity which He would find offensive? Is there *anything* which would cause Him to become angry? Or is He indifferent no matter what people choose to do?

In considering ancient religions which were characterized by idol worship, it is easy to think modern day religions are somehow different. But this is mistaken for two reasons. First, there are cultures existing today which still worship idols. Second, as previously noted, even if a modern day religion does not consider gods as mystically present in an idol, all religions constitute a *conception* of God, a *mental* image of the nature and character of God and His relationship to man. And that conception forms the basis of your entire worldview.

> **Your conception of God is a ruling, controlling factor in your everyday life. From that conception flows your views regarding life, death, the hereafter, the sanctity of life, right and wrong, sexuality, wisdom, prayer, religious rites, and divine intervention.**

Chapter 3

What do you mean by "God"?

The nature and character of God as taught by Jesus Christ is founded upon the Bible.

For thousands of years man has pondered the existence and nature of God. Listing all the different beliefs would require thousands of volumes of books. Consider just a few of these views.

There is no personal God of any kind.

There is no personal God, but rather a universal energy and force that animates us all.

God is the collective consciousness of the human race.

There are several spirit beings who have power over different aspects of life and the universe — a sun god, a rain god, a fertility god, a god of war, and others.

There are gods and goddesses as described in the ancient civilizations of …

God created everything, but He does not concern Himself with man's affairs and we can't know Him.

There are gods and goddesses, and they are revealed through the writings in the Vedas and the teachings of Hinduism.

God is revealed through the writings in the Koran and the teachings of Islam.

There is a personal God who has revealed Himself in all religions — each is true and each leads to God.

In John 3:16 where we are told "*God* so loved the world," which (if any) of these definitions are we talking about? A universal force? A collective consciousness? A host of spirit beings? The gods of the Mayans? Incas? Vikings? The gods of fallen ancient empires such as the Egyptians? Babylonians? Assyrians? Romans? Greeks? The gods of a specific, modern day Indian tribe in the Amazon rain forest? A particular Eskimo tribe in the polar regions? A nomadic Bedouin tribe in the desert? As pointed out in the previous chapter, the gods (or God) in each of these groups had their own nature and characteristics. Which concept of God is in view?

The nature and character of God as understood through Jesus Christ requires a detailed study of the Bible. For it is in the Bible that God reveals Himself to mankind through the writings of His prophets, apostles, and Christ Himself. It is outside the scope of this book to address the authority of the Bible or the principles that should be used in its interpretation. Our goal in this book is to grasp foundational truths regarding the word "God" as taught by Jesus Christ who Himself held to the inspiration and authority of scripture. In doing so we will understand the full import of the phrase "*God* so loved the world.

> Your conception of God is just one of many throughout the history of the world. That conception may have been formed by your parents, the teachings of a philosopher, the sayings of a wise man, the sacred writings of a religion outside Christianity, or any number of other sources. But the message of John 3:16 pertains to the teachings of Jesus Christ, and He held to the authority of Old Testament prophets, Himself, and the apostles He commissioned. If your understanding of the nature and character of God does not align with scripture, your disagreement is ultimately with Jesus Christ who boldly declared "I am ... the truth" JOHN 14:6.

Chapter 4

There is One God

The many conceptions of God throughout history are not equally valid, for there is only one God.

In the ancient way of thinking, victory in war did not necessarily mean the gods of the opposing army did not exist, but simply that they were less powerful. And in similar manner, the defeated army did not interpret defeat as necessarily meaning their own gods did not exist, but simply that they had displeased them in some way or the gods of the opposing army were more powerful. This mindset is evident in the historical account of an official of the Assyrian empire taunting an Israelite king named Hezekiah. In the presence of the Israelite army, the Assyrian official said:

> *Beware that Hezekiah does not mislead you, saying, "The* Lord *will deliver us." <u>Has any one of the gods of the nations delivered his land from the hand of the king of Assyria?</u> Where are the gods of Hamath and Arpad? Where are the gods of Sepharvaim? And when have they delivered Samaria from my hand? <u>Who among all the gods of these lands have delivered</u>*

> *their land from my hand, that the* LORD *would deliver Jerusalem from my hand?* ISAIAH 36:18–20

Hamath, Arpad, Sepharvaim and Samaria were lands that had suffered defeat by the Assyrian empire, and reference is made to the "gods of these lands" being unable to effect deliverance. So in the ancient way of thinking, the common perception was numerous gods existed. They *all* were real, even those of other nations.

This worldview of there being multiple gods is in direct contradiction to the teachings of Jesus Christ. When it is stated "For *God* so loved the world," the God being referred to is not one god amidst a host of other gods, but rather the only true God who alone has existence.

God Himself affirms He is the only God. In numerous places God says of Himself:

> *I am He, And there is no god besides Me.* DEUTERONOMY 32:39

> *For I am God, and there is no other; I am God, and there is no one like Me.* ISAIAH 46:9

> *There is no one like Me in all the earth.* EXODUS 9:14

> *I am the* LORD, *and there is no other; Besides Me there is no God.* ISAIAH 45:5

> *I am He. Before Me there was no God formed, and there will be none after Me.* ISAIAH 43:10

> *Is there any God besides Me, Or is there any other Rock? I know of none.* ISAIAH 44:8

These statements clearly indicate the uniqueness of God. There never has and never will be anyone who can even compare to Him. He has absolutely no equal.

There being only one God is the basis for God's prohibitions against worshiping other gods. It did not matter how elaborate the religious system, how imposing the idol, or how impressive the temple architecture. If these were representative of a false god, they were not to be honored, feared, or in any way regarded as God. Countless times this was commanded.

> *I am the* Lord *your God ... You shall have no other gods before Me.* Exodus 20:2–3

> *You shall not follow other gods, any of the gods of the peoples who surround you.* Deuteronomy 6:14

> *Let there be no strange god among you; Nor shall you worship any foreign god.* Psalm 81:9

> *I am the* Lord *your God; you shall not fear the gods of the Amorites.* Judges 6:10

> *Do not go after other gods to serve them and to worship them.* Jeremiah 25:6

> *You shall not fear other gods, nor bow down yourselves to them nor serve them nor sacrifice to them.* 2 Kings 17:35

The world is filled with monuments, temples, altars and artifacts that different cultures have used in the worship of their gods. Some of these are still in use today. As architecturally impressive and historically interesting as these sites may be, it must be understood they represent religious systems that

God prohibited because they perpetrated a false conception of Himself.

There are two serious implications of there being only one God, and they are startling.

There is only one true God, so all conceptions of God outside of Jesus Christ are false and represent gods that do not even exist. This is critical, for it is substantially different from not only ancient thoughts of God but even some contemporary viewpoints.

It is not that the gods of another religion have actual existence, and the God of Jesus Christ is more powerful, more knowledgeable, and so on. The other gods throughout history and in the present day *are not even there*. They are *not real*. They *do not exist*. It does not matter what image was used in the worship of the god. It does not even matter if the god in the particular religion was represented by any idol at all. There is in reality only *one* God.

Since there is only one true God, it is He who determines right and wrong, what are appropriate acts of worship, how to pray, and all other things related to religious life. The rites associated with the different gods in different religions are not equally valid. And as such there necessarily follows this second inescapable conclusion:

All activities, services, and worldviews based on a conception of God outside of Jesus Christ are ultimately vain. As previously shown, a man's conception of God has implications on every aspect of life. These different conceptions affect his view of right and wrong, the sanctity of life, what happens after death, and other important issues. People may strictly adhere to the teachings of their religion in accordance with their particular god. They may faithfully fulfill all the religious rites, daily prayers, and acts of worship prescribed. The code of conduct in the religion may be very strict by insisting on various activities of self-denial, and they may honor them all. But ultimately, if they are doing these things for a god other than the God of Jesus Christ, that god does not hear. And it is not that the god is unwilling to hear, it is that he has no ears to hear. It was the recognition of this futility that drove those who knew Jesus Christ to exclaim to those who were given to the worship of other gods:

> *You should turn from these vain things [lifeless idols] to a living God, who made the heaven and the earth and the sea and all that is in them.* ACTS 14:15

Note how scripture describes the idols themselves, and the worship and service associated with them: it is "vain." It is empty, void of result, worthless, and serves no purpose. And this exhortation still applies today.

> **God Himself affirms He is the only true God. There is absolutely no one like Him. He forbids the worship of others gods because they are not real and do not even exist; they are false gods. And they are as false as the idols carved out of stone from ancient civilizations. Your service to any god other than the God of Jesus Christ is ultimately empty, and serves no purpose. There is only one true God, and it is the God of Jesus Christ.**

CHAPTER 5

God Created and Sustains All Things

All that is, whether visible or invisible, was created by God.

Compared to where man was thousands of years ago, we have come a long way in understanding the world in which we live. Through advances in technology we observe both the minute and the enormous, the infinitesimally small and the astronomically large at deeper and deeper levels. But irrespective of advances in science, one thing is self-evident and inwardly known by every man, even though he may suppress this irrefutable truth.

The physical universe and all the complexity within it did not come to exist out of absolute nothingness. From the vast expanse of space filled with innumerable galaxies which themselves contain countless stars and planets, to the minute, intricate subatomic particles of which these massive objects are comprised, to the diverse and complex forms of life that exist on earth — these all did not ultimately come from absolutely nothing. The processes we observe in the world, and the objects involved within those processes, had a starting point.

God created all things. Everything that exist, and every process surrounding those things on both a macro and micro level, is the handiwork of an exceedingly creative, intelligent, all powerful, eternal God. The planets which orbit the sun in their orderly patterns; the ability of certain insects and sea creatures to mimic their environment and change color so as to avoid detection; the instinct of birds to gather twigs and build a protective nest to hatch and feed their young; the ability of plants to produce seeds and thereby perpetuate themselves from year to year; this is all the creative work of God.

> *In the beginning <u>God created the heavens and the earth</u>.* GENESIS 1:1

> *<u>You created all things</u>, and because of Your will they existed and were created.* REVELATION 4.11

> *It is <u>You who have made the heaven and the earth and the sea, and all that is in them</u>.* ACTS 4:24

> *For the* LORD *is a great God and a great King above all gods, in whose hand are the depths of the earth, the peaks of the mountains are His also. <u>The sea is His, for it was He who made it, and His hands formed the dry land</u>.* PSALM 95:3-5

> *The heavens are Yours, the earth also is Yours; The world and all it contains, <u>You have founded them</u>.* PSALM 89:11

> *The heavens are telling of the glory of God; And their expanse is declaring <u>the work of His hands</u>.* PSALM 19:1

The Nature and Character of God

> *Whatever the Lord pleases, He does, In heaven and in earth, in the seas and in all deeps. He causes the vapors to ascend from the ends of the earth; Who makes lightnings for the rain, Who brings forth the wind from His treasuries.* PSALM 135:6–7

> *Thus says the* LORD, *"Heaven is My throne and the earth is My footstool. Where then is a house you could build for Me? And where is a place that I may rest? For My hand made all these things, thus all these things came into being," declares the* LORD. ISAIAH 66:1-2

> *Give thanks to the Lord of lords ... To Him who made the heavens with skill ... To Him who spread out the earth above the waters ... To Him who made the great lights ... The sun to rule by day ... The moon and stars to rule by night.* PSALM 136:3–9

> *He who made the Pleiades and Orion And changes deep darkness into morning, Who also darkens day into night, Who calls for the waters of the sea And pours them out on the surface of the earth, The Lord is His name.* AMOS 5:8

And God's creative activity extends to man himself who was part of the creation.

> *God created man ... male and female He created them.* GENESIS 1:27

> *Then the Lord God formed man of dust from the ground, and breathed into his nostrils the breath of life; and man became a living being.* GENESIS 2:7

God Created and Sustains All Things

Creation is the basis God used to answer questions about human suffering. There was a man called Job who had lost his children, his wealth, and even his health. In the midst of this great physical and emotional agony, he was wanting answers as to why God was allowing him to go through such hardship. God humbled him by pointing to the wonders of His creation.

> *Where were you when <u>I laid the foundation of the earth</u>? Tell Me, if you have understanding, Who set its measurements? Since you know. Or who stretched the line on it? On what were its bases sunk? Or who laid its cornerstone ... Or who enclosed the sea with doors When, bursting forth, it went out from the womb; When <u>I made</u> a cloud its garment And thick darkness its swaddling band, And <u>I placed</u> boundaries on it And set a bolt and doors, And <u>I said</u>, "Thus far you shall come, but no farther; And here shall your proud waves stop"? Have you ever in your life commanded the morning, And caused the dawn to know its place, That it might take hold of the ends of the earth ... Have you entered into the springs of the sea Or walked in the recesses of the deep? Have the gates of death been revealed to you, Or have you seen the gates of deep darkness? Have you understood the expanse of the earth? Tell Me, if you know all this.* JOB 38:4–18

The passage above is a very small portion of God's answer to Job. God goes on to bring out numerous other creative acts. Such a message only has meaning if God is in fact the Creator of all things.

Some hold the universe and all life is the result of random processes over eons of time from matter that somehow formed from nothing. To put it another way, some hold all that is does not reflect the creative handiwork of an all powerful God — all that exist can or will eventually be explained by the laws of physics, biology, and other fields of study. It is not necessary to posit the existence of God from all that is seen.

Scripture stands in direct contraction to any position that denies God's creative role in the universe. If God chose never to engage in any creative act, then there would be absolute nothingness. But God did choose to act. He conceived in His mind all the galaxies, stars, vegetation, and life forms. And He acted on His thoughts, and hence all that is came to be.

God sustains all things. He is not only the reason all that is initially came into being. He is the reason things *continue* to exist after they initially had been created. Jesus said:

> *Consider the ravens, for they neither sow nor reap; they have no storeroom nor barn, and yet God feeds them.* LUKE 12:24

> *Observe how the lilies of the field grow; they do not toil nor do they spin ... God so clothes the grass of the field.* MATTHEW 6:28—30

And in the continuance of the human race through the procreative process and the provision of daily needs, God is at work.

> *For You formed my inward parts; You wove me in my mother's womb.* PSALM 139:13

> *Before I [the Lord] formed you in the womb I knew you.* JEREMIAH 1:5

God Created and Sustains All Things

> *He causes His sun to rise on the evil and the good, and sends rain on the righteous and the unrighteous.* MATTHEW 5:45

> *He did good and gave you rains from heaven and fruitful seasons, satisfying your hearts with food and gladness.* ACTS 14:17

> *He Himself gives to all people life and breath and all things; and He made from one man every nation of mankind to live on all the face of the earth, having determined their appointed times and the boundaries of their habitation.* ACTS 17:25-26.

> *In Him we live and move and exist.* ACTS 17:28

These two works of God — His creating and sustaining all things — are beautifully related in a Psalm. The writer is so inspired by these works that he begins by exalting God's majesty and greatness, saying "Bless the LORD, O my soul! You are very great." He then poetically describes God's awe inspiring creation as something which "clothes" Him with "splendor and majesty," expressing how God covers Himself with light "as with a cloak," stretched out heaven "like a tent curtain" and covered the earth with water "as with a garment."

> *Bless the LORD, O my soul! O LORD my God, You are very great; You are clothed with splendor and majesty, Covering Yourself with light as with a cloak, Stretching out heaven like a tent curtain. He lays the beams of His upper chambers in the waters; He makes the clouds His chariot; He walks upon the wings of the wind; He makes the winds His messengers, Flaming fire His ministers. He established the earth upon its*

The Nature and Character of God

> *foundations, So that it will not totter forever and ever. <u>You covered it with the deep</u> as with a garment; The waters were standing above the mountains. At <u>Your rebuke they fled, At the sound of Your thunder they hurried away.</u> The mountains rose; the valleys sank down To the place which <u>You established for them. You set a boundary that they may not pass over</u>, So that they will not return to cover the earth.* PSALM 104:1-9

The writer then reflects on God sustaining His creation by providing water which can "give drink" to animals, and allow the "grass" and "vegetation" to "grow" for the benefit of both man and beast.

> *<u>He sends forth</u> springs in the valleys; They flow between the mountains; They give drink to every beast of the field; The wild donkeys quench their thirst. Beside them the birds of the heavens dwell; They lift up their voices among the branches. <u>He waters the mountains from His upper chambers;</u> The earth is satisfied with the fruit of His works. <u>He causes the grass to grow</u> for the cattle, And vegetation for the labor of man, So that he may bring forth food from the earth, And wine which makes man's heart glad, So that he may make his face glisten with oil, And food which sustains man's heart. The trees of the* LORD *drink their fill, The cedars of Lebanon which He planted, Where the birds build their nests, And the stork, whose home is the fir trees. The high mountains are for the wild goats; The cliffs are a refuge for the shephanim.* PSALM 104:10–18

Next the writer reflects on the glory of the seasons of the year which God Himself established as part of creation.

God Created and Sustains All Things

> *He made the moon for the seasons; The sun knows the place of its setting. You appoint darkness and it becomes night, In which all the beasts of the forest prowl about. The young lions roar after their prey And seek their food from God. When the sun rises they withdraw And lie down in their dens. Man goes forth to his work And to his labor until evening. O* Lord, *how many are Your works! In wisdom You have made them all; The earth is full of Your possessions.*
> Psalm 104:19–24

Finally, the writer reflects on the mighty seas which are filled with life and depend on God's provision.

> *There is the sea, great and broad, In which are swarms without number, Animals both small and great. There the ships move along, And Leviathan, which You have formed to sport in it. They all wait for You To give them their food in due season. You give to them, they gather it up; You open Your hand, they are satisfied with good. You hide Your face, they are dismayed; You take away their spirit, they expire And return to their dust. You send forth Your Spirit, they are created; And You renew the face of the ground.* Psalm 104:25–30

This psalm is just one of many passages attributing glory to God for the awesomeness of His creation.

What we deem simple, common, everyday activities actually involve millions of exceedingly complicated, dependent, coordinated processes designed by God who created and sustains all things. Consider just one: your reading or listening to this paragraph. If reading, light is traveling through the air and being processed by your eye's complex optical system. If listening, sound waves are traveling and causing vibrations to your eardrum. This visual and audio stimuli is converted to signals which travel to your brain through various nerves. Your brain interprets those signals as words and sentences corresponding to thoughts and ideas — something that is nowhere near being understood. Through more exceedingly complex processes (which also are nowhere near being understood), your mind is able to evaluate those thoughts and ideas, associate them with memories, and identify relationships between them and other thoughts and ideas. All these activities involve extremely precise physiological processes working together and thereby allowing you to enjoy the faculty of comprehension. And this is without even considering the fact that if you can comprehend this paragraph, you are alive, and we still do not understand the mystery of human life.

> **God created you and has sustained you your entire life. The abilities you possess are there because He has willed that it be so. He has provided the food, water and shelter that has sustained you to this day. And all the beauty, complexity and wonder you see in creation are the works of His infinite, powerful, creative mind.**

Chapter 6

God has no Form

God is not comprised of any created thing, and no image can reflect the manner in which He exists.

There are two profound passages where God speaks of Himself in relation to His creation.

> *Thus says the* Lord, *"Heaven is My throne and the earth is My footstool.* <u>*Where then is a house you could build for Me? And where is a place that I may rest?*</u> *For My hand made all these things, thus all these things came into being," declares the* Lord. Isaiah 66:1-2

> *"Can a man hide himself in hiding places so I do not see him?" declares the* Lord. *"*<u>*Do I not fill the heavens and the earth?*</u>*" declares the* Lord. Jeremiah 23:24

In both these passages, several important truths about God can be observed.

The true God is not comprised of any created thing. When He says "My *hand* made all *these things*," He necessarily places Himself above and separate from all He created. His "hand"

The Nature and Character of God

is simply a figure of speech referring to His *creative will*. As we are told in another passage:

> *Worthy are You, our Lord and our God, to receive glory and honor and power; for <u>You created all things</u>, and because of <u>Your will</u> they existed, and were created.*
> **REVELATION 4:11**

In stating God is not made up of any created thing, all creation is meant, even that which the human eye cannot see.

The true God is not bound by any space. It is not as if He exist in a certain location over there, but not over here. Nor can He be thought of as capable of being contained in a certain area. When He says "Heaven is My throne and the earth is My footstool. Where then is a house you could build for Me?", He was not suggesting that He was some spiritual, unseen, intergalactic giant which if a house were built just a little bit bigger than the heavens and the earth, it would fit Him. The true God cannot be thought of as being *there*, but simply *being* — not as existing *there*, but simply *existing*.

The true God has no form. Man can conceive of a shape or form with no physical properties very easily. Myths and science fiction stories are filled with fictitious creatures, and each creature represents something that does not really exist — in reality it has no physical properties, but is simply imaginary. The creature *does* exist, however, as a *form* or *image;* that is why its shape can be drawn and its form described.

But not only does God have no material, physical properties, He has no *form*. There is *absolutely no shape* or *figure* that can be *conceived in one's mind* that reflects God, for He does not "look" like *anything*. It is not as if He exist in some other dimension, and if we just were in that dimension we would see Him. Nor is it that He can be conceived of as One who has a vague form, such as a vapor cloud. The true God has *no form*.

Previously it was shown that much of history involved the worship of idols; graven images from trees or stone that were regarded as images of the gods, and who were in some mystical way present in the object. But it was this tendency in man to think of God in this false way that caused Him to give this caution and prohibition:

> *So watch yourselves carefully, since <u>you did not see any form on the day the Lord spoke to you</u> … do not act corruptly and make a graven image for yourselves in the form of any figure, the likeness of male or female, the likeness of any animal that is on the earth, the likeness of any winged bird that flies in the sky, the likeness of anything that creeps on the ground, the likeness of any fish that is in the water below the earth. And beware not to lift up your eyes to heaven and see the sun and the moon and the stars, all the host of heaven, and be drawn away and worship them and serve them, those which the* Lord *your God has allotted to all the peoples under the whole heaven.*
> Deuteronomy 4:15-19

And in another place He gives a specific, direct prohibition:

> *<u>You shall not make for yourself an idol, or any likeness of what is in heaven above or on the earth beneath or in the water under the earth.</u> You shall not worship them or serve them.* Exodus 20:4-5

The Nature and Character of God

The true God cannot be conceived of as having any form, bound by any space, nor comprised of any created thing visible or invisible. No image or shape conceived in the mind represents Him. It does not matter how beautiful the form, how artistic the image, or how awe inspiring the picture; it does not accurately portray Him, and is not to be worshiped.

God's prohibition of images is not necessarily a prohibition of figurative representations. Psalm 34:7 says "How precious is Your lovingkindness, O God! And the children of men take refuge in the shadow of Your wings." This verse obviously brings to mind a mental image of the vulnerable being protected by wings, and it is used for poetic effect. Even so, a pictorial representation which mirrored this verse could be used for artistic effect, and neither the poetic phrase nor the artistic image need be viewed as asserting God has literal wings.

When on a clear, starry night one gazes into the vastness of space, a sense of wonder enters the human heart over the awesomeness of it all. But when beholding that boundless creation, we are not looking at God, but rather at the handiwork of Him who exists in an incomprehensible way. It is not as if the universe is a huge interstellar bubble, and if we could just travel far enough, we would reach the end, penetrate the bubble, and there God would be. Nor are other conceptions of God's existence accurate — being present in another dimension in a form we just cannot see, and the like.

> **In the true God, we are dealing with a Being whose mode of existence is beyond anything we experience or understand — consisting of no created thing and possessing no form.**

CHAPTER 7

God is Always There

God is not limited or confined to any one place, and He personally witnesses everything we do.

Man understands the world around him within a spatial orientation — going there, being here, coming from that place, and so on. Yes, through the use of technology such as cameras one man can witness activities in numerous locations simultaneously. But even then he himself is still only in one place.

So where is God as respects location? Where can He be found? We have noted in a previous chapter that ultimately God cannot be thought of as being *here*, but simply *being*; not as existing *there*, but simply *existing*. He is not comprised of any physical matter, nor does He possesses any form. So where is He? The answer is just as obtuse.

God is always there. Darkness does not hide one from Him; walls or locked doors do not block His access; and running or fleeing does not distance oneself from Him. There is no place a man can go where God is not there. Concerning Himself God says:

The Nature and Character of God

> *"Can a man hide himself in hiding places so I do not see him?" declares the* LORD. *"Do I not fill the heavens and the earth?" declares the* LORD. JEREMIAH 23:24

And when contemplating God being ever present, David poetically states:

> *Where can I go from Your Spirit? Or where can I flee from Your presence? If I ascend to heaven, You are there; If I make my bed in Sheol [hell], behold, You are there. If I take the wings of the dawn, if I dwell in the remotest part of the sea, even there Your hand will lead me, And Your right hand will lay hold of me. If I say, "Surely the darkness will overwhelm me, and the light around me will be night," even the darkness is not dark to You, And the night is as bright as the day. Darkness and light are alike to You.* PSALM 139:7-12

When David was determined to build a temple for God, He was told:

> *Thus says the* LORD, *"Heaven is My throne and the earth is My footstool. Where then is a house you could build for Me? And where is a place that I may rest? For My hand made all these things, thus all these things came into being," declares the* LORD. ISAIAH 66:1-2

So where is God? Once again, we are dealing with a Being whose mode of existence is far above all human comprehension. God is separate from His creation, and yet He is always there. If God never chose to engage in any creative act, He would exist in the void of absolute nothingness as a conscious, all powerful, loving Being with an infinite mind. And when He chose to create all things, He did not *change* that mode of existence. He still exist as a conscious, all powerful, loving Being with an infinite mind. He was in no way displaced, confined, or limited by His own creation.

The perspectives of man and God are as far apart as the heavens are from the earth. From our perspective as created beings, our experience is limited to understanding the world through spatial limitations God Himself imposed — geographical markers such as compass coordinates and height elevations along with dimensions of depth, width and height. But from God's perspective no such limitations ever existed in relation to Himself either before or after the creation. So the very question "*Where* is God *located?*" is seeking an answer to something that ultimately never had any relevance to God to begin with. It is similar to a fish asking "What part of the ocean did you hatch in?" That question is reasonable from a fish to another fish, but not from a fish to a man.

God being always there means He witnesses everything as if He were observing it in person. There are different levels of awareness as respects knowing something. We can become aware of a certain act or event by reading about it, hearing the audio from it, or watching a video of it. But witnessing an event while being present provides an even deeper level of awareness. And it is this level of awareness, and more, which God has of mankind because He is always there.

> *There is <u>no creature hidden</u> from His sight, but all things are <u>open and laid bare</u> to the eyes of Him with whom we have to do.* HEBREWS 4:13

> *The eyes of the* LORD *are in <u>every place</u>, Watching the evil and the good.* PROVERBS 15:3

God is intimately aware of all our deeds for He witnessed them. This has positive and negative implications. On the negative side, we all have done things we think no one knows about; things we would be ashamed to have others discover; things we would rather not confess but keep concealed. But the truth is nothing is concealed because *God* was there. *He* witnessed it in person. We may have been careful to make sure our actions were not discovered. We may have taken steps to hide and cover our tracks. But God not only witnessed our initial act, but every subsequent step we took to cover things up. It does not matter if the deed was committed in the day or in the night, whether we disguised ourselves or acted with sleight of hand. It does not even matter if we were successful in avoiding getting caught. *God* saw it all.

On the positive side, God personally witnessed the injustices we have been subjected to from others, as well as all the suffering life has brought our way. Wrongdoers may seem to have gotten away with things, and they may indeed live their lives without being exposed. But before God they have always been exposed, and their works never concealed. *God* knows our innocence! And when we have gone through our darkest hours with physical suffering brought on by an illness, accident or other catastrophe, God witnessed that also. *He was there.*

God being present everywhere means He is never inaccessible on account of where we are. We may think if we are to have an encounter with God we must go to a mountain top or some other scenic location. Scenic views are definitely inspiring, but God is as accessible from a mountain top as He is everywhere else. Hospital beds, prisons, or court rooms do not bar His presence. Rulers cannot send Him into exile.

Managers cannot expel Him. And corrupt establishments cannot forbid Him entry.

> **God is separate from His creation and yet always there. He has personally witnessed and observed you from the time of your infancy, and will continue to do so every single day from now until you take your last breath. And throughout your whole life, His accessibility has never been nor ever will be contingent on the physical location of where you are.**

Chapter 8

God is Eternal

God has no beginning and no end, and there is no cause for His existence — He always has been.

Man understands the world around him with a time orientation — departing here at that time, arriving there at that hour, and so on. There is the past, present and future, and these three never overlap. With man and with all created things there also is a point of origin; a time prior to which we did not exist.

What does God say of Himself in relation to time? As respects His origin, the answer is clear.

God has no beginning and no end. There never was a time when He did not exist, nor will there ever be a time where He ceases to exist. Scripture is replete with references affirming this fact.

> *Your throne is established from of old; <u>You are from everlasting</u>.* Psalm 93:2

> *Thus says the* Lord *... "<u>I am the first and I am the last</u>, And there is no God besides Me."* Isaiah 44:6

God is Eternal

> *"I am the Alpha and the Omega," says the Lord God, "who is and who was and who is to come, the Almighty."* REVELATION 1:8

> *Of old You founded the earth, And the heavens are the work of Your hands. Even they will perish, but You endure; And all of them will wear out like a garment; Like clothing You will change them and they will be changed. But You are the same, And Your years will not come to an end.* PSALM 102:25–27

> *For thus says the high and exalted One Who lives forever.* ISAIAH 57:15

> *He who is the blessed and only Sovereign, the King of kings and Lord of lords, who alone possesses immortality.* 1 TIMOTHY 6:15–16

With these scriptures we are once again faced with an incomprehensible truth completely outside human experience. Everything we observe in life can be traced to some cause — such and such happened because of this, which is the result of that, which is a consequence of this, and on and on its goes. But with God it is not possible to trace an origin. He always has been, and always will be.

Some questions posed about God have no relevance because we are asking the question from our own finite, cause and effect, time-oriented framework. Questions such as "*Where* did God come from?" "*How* did God come into existence?" or "*When* did God come to be" all fall into this category. There is *no one* like God; *no one*. His mode of existence is completely outside human experience. Because *we* cannot conceive of a Being having no origin does not mean such a Being cannot exist. It just means *we* are *not* like *Him*.

God being eternal is related to His name "I Am." To truly process the significance of this name, it must be considered in light of Hebrew culture.

In Hebrew proper names were often ascribed based on some characteristic or surrounding circumstance of the object in view. Thus Hagar named the place where God had observed her distress and provided comfort "You are a God who sees" (GENESIS 16:14). When the patriarch Abraham laughed at God's message that his barren wife would have a son, God had him name his son "He laughs" (GENESIS 17:19). And Isaac and Rebekah named their son Esau's twin brother "heel catcher" because at birth he came forth with his hand holding onto Esau's heel (GENESIS 17:25-26).

God revealed His name in the midst of calling Moses to divine service, and that name must be understood in this Hebrew context. Moses asked God "What is your name?" This was tantamount to asking "What word or words are descriptive of who You are?" God replied His name was "I Am," something that can viewed as meaning "He who exist" (EXODUS 3:13-14). To us this seems like a very odd name, but it perfectly reflects the eternality of God. God "is."

> **There is no cause for why God is, and no reason for who He is. He is who He is, and He always has been and always will be.**

Chapter 9

God is All-Knowing

God knows what has been, is now, and will be, as well as what could have been.

God knows everything with perfect knowledge, and there is absolutely nothing He does not know.

God knows <u>all</u> things. 1 John 3:20

And scripture details at least five subdivisions under the "all things" that God knows.

God knows our hearts. He knows the thoughts we conceive, the imaginations we entertain, the desires in our hearts, and the motives behind every action.

You, Lord, <u>who know the hearts of all men</u> … Acts 1:24

<u>You know when I sit down and when I rise up</u>; You understand my thought from afar. You scrutinize my path … and are <u>intimately acquainted with all my ways</u>. Even before there is a word on my tongue, behold, O Lord, <u>You know it all</u>. Psalm 139:2-4

> *God sees not as man sees, for man looks at the outward appearance, but <u>the Lord looks at the heart</u>.* 1 SAMUEL 16:7
>
> *<u>The Lord searches all hearts</u>, and understands every intent of the thoughts.* 1 CHRONICLES 28:9

There are also numerous places where God directly speaks of what He knows about specific people or people groups.

> *<u>I know that in the integrity of your heart you have done this</u>.* GENESIS 20:6
>
> *<u>I know their intent</u> which they are developing today.* DEUTERONOMY 31:21
>
> *<u>I know your sitting down</u> And your going out and your coming in And your raging against Me.* ISAIAH 37:28
>
> *<u>I know that you are obstinate</u>, And your neck is an iron sinew And your forehead bronze.* ISAIAH 48:4
>
> *<u>I know their works and their thoughts</u>.* ISAIAH 66:18
>
> *<u>I know your transgressions</u> are many and your sins are great.* AMOS 5:12

And in the days of Noah, when the whole world was exceedingly corrupt, God made an assessment of the heart of every person on the face of the earth.

> *Then the <u>Lord saw</u> that the wickedness of man was great on the earth, and that <u>every intent of the thoughts of his heart</u> was only evil continually.* GENESIS 6:5

God knowing our hearts means He knows us at a level no other person can possibly know. In human interaction there are varied ways of communication: words, the intonation of words, eye movements, facial expressions, and gestures. Most of the time these reflect what is going on in our hearts, but not always. But God knows our true feelings behind every one of our outward expressions.

God knows us better than we know ourselves. Sometimes we react in a way that surprises us, and we do not understand our own actions. Our heart can also unjustly condemn us at times. But God knows all the dynamics that play into every thing we ever do. Nothing is ever a surprise to Him, and He knows all things.

God knows the future. This truth can be shown from scripture in multiple ways. First, the ability to know the future is what God Himself says is His unique, identifying trait.

> *I am God, and there is no other; I am God, and there is no one like Me, <u>declaring the end from the beginning, and from ancient times things which have not been done</u>.* ISAIAH 46:9-10

> *Who is like Me? Let him proclaim and declare it; Yes, let him recount it to Me in order, From the time that I established the ancient nation. And <u>let them declare to them the things that are coming. And the events that are going to take place</u>.* ISAIAH 44:7

Second, God's ability to know the future was the basis for testing who were His prophets in the Old Testament. A genuine prophet would be able to accurately predict those future events God had revealed to him. So God gave specific instructions on how to know the true prophet from the false prophet.

> *You may say in your heart, "How will we know the word which the* LORD *has not spoken?" When a prophet speaks in the name of the* LORD, <u>*if the thing does not come about or come true, that is the thing which the Lord has not spoken.*</u> *The prophet has spoken it presumptuously; you shall not be afraid of him.* DEUTERONOMY 18:21–22

Third, God knowing the future is shown by actual predictions that came to pass. The Old Testament contains many such prophecies, the majority of which have already been fulfilled. God specifically told Abram what the future held for his descendants (the nation of Israel), detailing their enslavement, eventual deliverance and return to a specific land.

> *God said to Abram, "Know for certain that your descendants will be strangers in a land that is not theirs, where they will be enslaved and oppressed four hundred years. But I will also judge the nation whom they will serve, and afterward they will come out with many possessions. As for you, you shall go to your fathers in peace; you will be buried at a good old age. Then in the fourth generation they will return here."* GENESIS 15:13–16

And the prophecies of Daniel are also very specific, detailing the rise and fall of several empires in relation to Israel.

> *Behold, three more kings are going to arise in Persia. Then a fourth will gain far more riches than all of them; as soon as he becomes strong through his riches, he will arouse the whole empire against the realm of Greece. And a mighty king will arise, and he will rule with great authority and do as he pleases. But as soon*

as he has arisen, his kingdom will be broken up and parceled out toward the four points of the compass, though not to his own descendants, nor according to his authority which he wielded, for his sovereignty will be uprooted and given to others besides them. Then the king of the South will grow strong, along with one of his princes who will gain ascendancy over him and obtain dominion; his domain will be a great dominion indeed. After some years they will form an alliance. DANIEL 11:2–6

Who but God alone could give details such as this before they come to pass? No wonder Daniel exclaimed during another vision "there is a God in heaven who reveals mysteries" (DANIEL 2:28).

God knows how things would have played out under different circumstances. In any situation there are an infinite number of hypotheticals; a countless number of variables that could have been changed. God's knowledge is so vast, He knows how each and every one of those imaginary situations would have played out even though they never actually took place.

David was in the midst of making a critical life and death decision. He was on the run from those who were determined to kill him, and he needed to know what would happen if he ventured into a city named Keilah and sought refuge. David asked the Lord "Will the men of Keilah surrender me?" and the Lord replied "They will surrender you." As a result, David never ventured into the city. God spared David's life by telling him something that never actually took place, but would have taken place in another scenario (1 SAMUEL 23:9-13).

God knows our needs. When Jesus gave a teaching on prayer, He pointed out this simple and profound truth:

> *[God] knows what you need before you ask Him.*
> MATTHEW 6:8.

This statement is not suggesting it is wrong to ask God for daily sustenance. Jesus Himself taught such a request should characterize one's prayer life (MATTHEW 6:11). It is simply that our request should be made with the understanding God knows our needs. It is not as if we need to inform Him of something He does not know.

God knows Himself. He knows His thoughts, His desires, His plans, and His own nature and character. God knows Himself perfectly. Of Himself God says:

> *For I know the plans that I have.* JEREMIAH 29:11
>
> *I take no pleasure in the death of the wicked.* EZEKIEL 33:11

When God makes these statements, He makes them about what pleases Him and grieves Him. And He makes these statements with perfect knowledge of His eternal, unchanging character.

There are statements God makes that presuppose He not only knows Himself, but He necessarily knows everything about everyone else.

> *I am God, and there is no other; I am God, and there is no one like Me.* ISAIAH 46:9

The only way God could positively say "There is no one like Me" is if He not only knew Himself, but He knew everybody else who has existed, exist now, and will exist. And in another place He says:

> *"For <u>My thoughts are not your thoughts, Nor are your ways My ways</u>," declares the* LORD*. "For as the heavens are higher than the earth, So are <u>My ways higher than your ways And My thoughts than your thoughts</u>."*
> ISAIAH 55:8–9

Once again, this verse necessitates God knowing not only Himself, but everyone else. That is why He can draw a contrast between His thoughts and ways and man's thoughts and ways.

In another place, God related an exceedingly important trait about Himself.

> *Then the word of the* LORD *came to me saying ... "At one moment I might speak concerning a nation or concerning a kingdom to uproot, to pull down, or to destroy it; if that nation against which I have spoken turns from its evil, <u>I will relent</u> concerning the calamity I planned to bring on it. Or at another moment I might speak concerning a nation or concerning a kingdom to build up or to plant it; if it does evil in My sight by not obeying My voice, then <u>I will think better of the good with which I had promised</u> to bless it."* JEREMIAH 18:5–10

God can speak this way because He knows Himself, and how He will react to sinful men. He may be determined to destroy a sinful nation, but will relent of bringing calamity if they turn. Likewise He may be minded to bless a nation, but will relent of that blessing if they rebel.

God knows Himself so well, He knows with absolute certainty how He would react in a hypothetical situation that does not actually take place. This is clear in a message given to the prophet Ezekiel when ancient Israel was in a season of dark rebellion.

> *Then the word of the* LORD *came to me saying, "Son of man, if a country sins against Me by committing unfaithfulness, and I stretch out My hand against it, destroy its supply of bread, send famine against it and cut off from it both man and beast, <u>even though these three men, Noah, Daniel and Job were in its midst,</u> by their own righteousness <u>they could only deliver themselves,</u>" declares the Lord* GOD. EZEKIEL 14:12–14

Noah, Daniel and Job were godly men, and here God details how He would react if they were to intercede on Israel's behalf. Only God can speak with such certainty about Himself.

> **God knows every thought, imagination, desire, and motive you have ever had and will have. He knows the sorrows, injustices and pain you yourself have suffered, as well as those you have subjected others to. He knows the outcome of every conceivable decision you will ever make. He knows what your future holds. He knows where you stand in relation to Himself. He knows how He Himself will react to you in light of that standing. And He knows your immediate reaction to these facts.**

Chapter 10

God is All-Wise

God being wise means He orders and arranges all things with great ingenuity.

A classic illustration of wisdom is the story of king Solomon settling a quarrel between two prostitutes over an infant. Each woman had recently given birth, but one of the infants had died, and each woman claimed the living infant was her own and accused the other of lying. Solomon responded by voicing an order to cut the baby in two and give each woman half. One woman pleaded with the king to spare the infant's life and give the child to the other, while the other agreed the baby should be divided and neither should have it. Solomon obviously did not have the order carried out, but simply gave the infant to the woman who pleaded for the child's life knowing she was actually the mother. The story spread among the people of the land, and they revered king Solomon "for they saw that the wisdom of God was in him to administer justice" (1 KINGS 3:16-28).

Solomon's actions are rightly viewed as wise because they reveal not only insight and discernment into human nature — he knew the true mother would want to spare the infant's life — but also ingenuity and cleverness in bringing out that fact. And that wisdom is also rightly viewed as having its origin in God, for it is He who is all-wise.

God is exceedingly wise, but unlike Solomon it is never with the goal to uncover something unknown. God is ingenious because that is who He is by nature, so everything He does reflects that ingenuity and cleverness.

God's wisdom is revealed through the variety, creativity, and cleverness within creation. When taking into account man, animals, sea creatures, insects, plants, micro-organisms, etc., there are literally *millions* of different forms of life. Man constitutes just *one* form or species. And each of these life forms is exceedingly complex. Each has different methods of locomotion: flying, swimming, walking, hopping, scooting, slithering, jet propulsion, and crawling. Each has its own means of being aware of its surroundings: seeing, hearing, smelling, tasting, touching or sensing some form of vibration. Each has its own way of obtaining and processing the food, water and nutrients necessary for survival. Each has its own way of eliminating waste. Each has its own way of reproduction. Each has its own built-in instincts for its own survival. Each has an exceedingly complex physical form with intricately designed parts which coordinate with each other to accomplish all these things.

There is an interdependence between all these millions of forms of life, and even lifeless things play a vital role in their survival. Man needs vegetation, and plants are pollinated by animals, insects and other plants. All these life forms exist on an earth which itself has complex processes, and a sun which is an astrophysical marvel. The chemical and atomic processes involved in the sun continually producing light,

God is All-Wise

the atmosphere repeatedly forming rain-producing clouds, and the air continuously being replenished with oxygen are astonishing. And this is without even considering the wonder of the change of seasons, the rising and falling of the tides, and the cycles of days, months, and years.

To make God's creation even more astounding, it must be realized that within everything mentioned thus far there are numerous levels, subcategories, and divisions. Sea creatures do not just swim, they have different types of fins to help them swim — some to propel them on the ocean floor, and others with multiple fins which provide quick and outstanding maneuverability. Animals do not just have eyes, they have different types of eyes — some suited for seeing at night, and others for seeing long distances. And animals do not just have body parts, these body parts work in coordination with one another. For example, an eagle's wing or claw is comprised of muscles and joints working in perfect union with the eye and brain, allowing the eagle to see its prey, swoop, extend its claws, and grasp its prey with great precision. But that is just the eagle. There are muscles, tendons, joints, eyes, and brains in other animals that provide great speed, the application of great force, or extreme sensitivity to their surroundings. There are also highly complicated systems of equilibrium in man and animals allowing them to run while remaining upright and avoid falling over.

But we can move from the visible realm of what we normally see to that which can only be seen with the aid of technology from microscopes and telescopes. If we look inward, the different life forms are comprised of complex molecules, which are made up of atoms, which consist of particles, and on and on it goes. And if we go the opposite direction and expand our view outward, these life forms live on earth, which belongs to a solar system, which is part of a galaxy, which is within a galaxy cluster, and on and on it goes.

When contemplating the idea that one God created and sustains all these complex life forms, systems and processes on a sub-atomic and universal level, it reveals the many other traits of God we explore in this and other chapters. The human mind cannot fully grasp and track everything involved in just *one* life form, yet alone *millions* of life forms. But God's mind is so great, His creativity so vast, His intelligence so high, His powers so immense, His wisdom so deep, His knowledge so extensive, and His care so thoughtful that He conceived in His own mind all these life forms, systems, processes, dependencies, and relationships, and acted on His thoughts by creating and sustaining everything that has, or ever will, exist. Is it any wonder we read:

> *O* LORD, *how many are Your works!* In wisdom You have made them all. PSALM 104:24
>
> *It is He who made the earth by His power,* Who established the world by His wisdom; *And by His understanding He has stretched out the heavens.* JEREMIAH 10:12

God's wisdom is revealed through incorporating man's rebellion into fulfilling His own noble purposes. Men are capable of doing great evil; of doing what God does *not* want them to do. But God, who knows all things, orders man's affairs in a way that man's wrongdoing actually works towards a good end. This does not mean God conceived the evil thought and placed it into man's heart, or that He morally approves of the wrong committed, or that He takes pleasure in the evil act. It simply means that God — for reasons He deems good, right and just — decrees a noble outcome and appoints men who stubbornly defy Him as a means to obtain that noble end. He does not overrule man's evil plans, but as one who knows all things He incorporates those evil plans that have their origin in man to work towards a good end that originated in Himself.

If God using man's evil decisions to work for good seems hard to understand, we can realize that as fallen human beings we can do the same thing in a very limited way. A narcotics agent may allow a drug deal to proceed not because he approves of people using drugs, but because he wants to capture not only the drug dealer but also the supplier. A father may allow his daughter to continue to act deceptively and privately rebel against his command. But the father may do this not because he is unaware or approves of her deceitfulness, but rather with a view to let her reap the consequences of her actions and learn from her mistake. Of course these analogies have their limitations when applied to God, but they nonetheless do provide a glimpse into the dynamics going on.

The classic biblical example of God using man's rebellion for good is the true story of the Pharaoh of Egypt in the days of the prophet Moses. The nation of Israel was in bondage to the Egyptians at that time, serving as slaves under harsh, brutal, oppressive conditions. God through Moses commanded Pharaoh to let the Israelites go under threat of plague. Pharaoh refused, and God followed through on the threat and subjected Egypt to a miraculous and devastating plague. This cycle repeated itself with Pharaoh often asking the plague to be lifted while in the midst of it, only to harden his heart afterwards and refuse to let the Israelites go. After ten plagues Pharaoh finally agreed and freed the Israelites EXODUS 1-12.

The Nature and Character of God

When reflecting on the story of Israel's deliverance, it appears Pharaoh was frustrating the plan of God. After all, God was commanding one thing, and Pharaoh was rebelling against that command. It appears God's purposes were not playing out.

But Pharaoh's rebellion was part of God's plan.

God had a word for this arrogant leader of the most powerful nation in the world. God pointed out it was within His power to completely annihilate Pharaoh and his people. The only reason God tolerated Pharaoh's rebellion was to fulfill a higher purpose, and He even let Pharaoh know what it was.

> *For if by now I had put forth My hand and struck you and your people with pestilence, you would then have been cut off from the earth. But, indeed, <u>for this reason I have allowed you to remain, in order to show you My power and in order to proclaim My name through all the earth</u>.* EXODUS 9:15–16

Pharaoh's repeated rebellion was serving a higher, divine purpose: revealing God's power and giving occasion for God's praise. It was this display of God's power that became a source of praise for generations in Israel. Many songs were composed, much poetry was written, the historical account was referenced numerous times, and God even had the Israelites mark the occasion with an annual celebration. God was not simply passively reacting to history as if Pharaoh's rebellion was something that caught God by surprise. God *appointed* Pharaoh in the scheme of human history, knowing beforehand his stubborn character, so as to use that stubbornness to accomplish His noble purpose.

God's wisdom and ingenuity has been openly displayed to you throughout your whole life. It has been evident every day through His marvelous creation. The sorrow, injustices and pain you have suffered from others, as well as that which you subjected others to, is being overruled by Him to fulfill a higher, noble purpose He Himself decreed from the foundation of the world. You may not always see what that noble purpose is in the midst of your suffering, but that does not mean no such purpose exist. It just means you are not Him, and you do not see as He sees.

Chapter 11

God is All-Powerful

God exercises His infinite power in keeping with what He deems good, just, loving, and kind.

We have all desired to change circumstances or outcomes for what we deemed would be better or just. We may have sought to see an illness cured, a broken object fixed, or an oppressor judged. We did not have the power to immediately effect these desired results so we took medicine in hope of curing the illness, employed tools to attempt a repair, or took steps to see the person who wronged us face justice. Often we would be successful in our endeavors, but not always. And even when we were successful it was not within the time frame we wanted, and it involved a great deal of frustration. Our will and efforts were hampered by things outside of us; by things beyond our control or power.

What can be said of God as respects His will and His power? Is *anything* ultimately outside His control? If He determines a certain thing should actually come to pass, does He encounter resistance outside of Himself? The answer is clear.

God is All-Powerful

God's power is infinite, and nothing is impossible with Him. He is not subject to restraints outside Himself. As scripture says:

> <u>Nothing will be impossible</u> with God. LUKE 1:37

If God so willed, He could cure an illness, raise the dead, stop the earth's rotation, or darken the sun. He could cause something that does not exist to materialize, and something that does exist cease to be. Nothing is too hard for Him.

God rules all things and does as He pleases. In keeping with His own purposes, He accomplishes that which He deems fitting.

> <u>Whatever the Lord pleases, He does, In heaven and in earth, in the seas and in all deeps.</u> PSALM 135:6

> But our God is in the heavens; <u>He does whatever He pleases.</u> PSALM 115:3

> For I am God, and there is no other; I am God, and there is no one like Me, Declaring the end from the beginning, And from ancient times things which have not been done, Saying, "<u>My purpose will be established, And I will accomplish all My good pleasure.</u>" ISAIAH 46:9–10

God's power is revealed through the vastness and immensity of His creation. As one writer in scripture testifies, God's "invisible attributes" of being an all powerful God have been "evident" or "clearly visible" since the creation. And these attributes are *understood* through "what has been made," namely, the created universe.

The Nature and Character of God

> *That which is known about God is evident within them; for God made it evident to them. For since the creation of the world His invisible attributes, <u>His eternal power and divine nature, have been clearly seen, being understood through what has been made.</u>*
> ROMANS 1:19–20

And another writer speaks poetically of the stellar heavens which tell of the mighty power and glory of God.

> *<u>The heavens are telling of the glory of God; And their expanse is declaring the work of His hands.</u> Day to day pours forth speech, And night to night reveals knowledge. There is no speech, nor are there words; Their voice is not heard. Their line has gone out through all the earth, And their utterances to the end of the world. In them He has placed a tent for the sun, Which is as a bridegroom coming out of his chamber; It rejoices as a strong man to run his course. Its rising is from one end of the heavens, And its circuit to the other end of them; And there is nothing hidden from its heat.* PSALM 19:1–6

One prophet exclaims:

> *Ah Lord GOD! Behold, <u>You have made the heavens and the earth by Your great power</u> and by Your outstretched arm! Nothing is too difficult for You.* JEREMIAH 32:17

And of Himself God says:

> *To whom then will you liken Me ...? Lift up your eyes on high And <u>see who has created these stars, The One who leads forth their host by number,</u> He calls them all by name; <u>Because of the greatness of His might and*

> *the strength of His power, Not one of them is missing.*
> ISAIAH 40:25–26

When one contemplates all the forces in the universe, it is absolutely astonishing. The power of one star such as the sun in our solar system is beyond comprehension. Whether it be considered from the gravitational, electromagnetic or nuclear perspective, the power is exceedingly immense.

And this is just our sun.

If you were to take the countless number of stars over all time and consider the combined power of them all, it defies any comprehensible form of measurement. But such is the power of almighty God.

God's power is incapable of being exhausted or even diminished. When considering creation one may think exercising the power to create the universe would in some way weaken God. But such is not the case. As it is written:

> *Do you not know? Have you not heard? The Everlasting God, the* LORD, *the Creator of the ends of the earth Does not become weary or tired. His understanding is inscrutable.* ISAIAH 40:28

The creation account is revealed in the book of Genesis. Over a period of several days, God engages in various forms of creative activity after which we are told He "rested." But this word should in no way be interpreted to mean God became weary, but simply that He ceased from the particular creative activity in view. God's power is infinite, inexhaustible, and knows no bounds.

God's power is only directed and limited by His other attributes. This is true with respect to everything in creation. Whether it be the sun giving light, the clouds sending forth rain or the earth producing fruit, it is God who is at work. And when it comes to catastrophes such as tornadoes, earthquakes, tsunamis, hurricanes, or plagues, these things take place not because God lacks the power to stop them or is indifferent towards the misery caused by them. Rather it is that God, in keeping with His just, righteous, wise character, determined the dynamics involved in those catastrophes play out to those devastating ends. Natural catastrophes were not part of God's original creation, and they do not have the ability to bring themselves into existence or sustain themselves. They occur because an all-powerful God determined they should be part of a world that is in rebellion against Him.

God's power is directed and limited by His other attributes in relation to man as well. In man, God created beings who are capable of defying His *moral* will. In such defiance, men are doing what God does *not* want them to do. But men can only follow through with such defiance as God wills to give them the breath and strength to do so. And God willing to grant that breath and strength in no way means He *morally* approved of the evil act or took pleasure in it. Rather it means for reasons in keeping with His just, righteous, wise character, *He* determined the *act* take place. So ultimately no matter how determined men may be to effect their evil schemes, it is ultimately God and not man who determines whether that scheme actually plays out.

Man cannot overpower God's decrees. An evil man may not view his actions as criminal, and he may resist being arrested and dragged to an earthly court. He may also disagree with the judge over the character of his evil actions, and the sentence pronounced against him. He may seek to escape his prison sentence or the death penalty by appealing to a higher court, bribing the judge, or overcoming those guarding him and escaping. But all such tactics would be futile against almighty God. As the King of kings there would be no higher court. As the righteous One He could not be bribed. And as the all powerful One, if He has determined there will be a day when every man will stand before Him to give account, then that day cannot be avoided. And if in that appearance God passes sentence, it is within His power to carry it out, and that sentence could not be evaded or resisted: there would be no escape. Of Himself God says:

> *There is no one who can deliver from My hand.*
> DEUTERONOMY 32:39

> *Even from eternity I am He, and there is none who can deliver out of My hand; I act and who can reverse it?* ISAIAH 43:13

And prophets and godly people say of God:

> *He does according to His will in the host of heaven And among the inhabitants of earth; And no one can ward off His hand Or say to Him, "What have You done?"* DANIEL 4:35

> *Those who contend with the Lord will be shattered.*
> 1 SAMUEL 2:10

> *Consider the work of God, For who is able to straighten what He has bent?* ECCLESIASTES 7:13

> *Power and might are in Your hand so that <u>no one can stand against You</u>.* 2 CHRONICLES 20:6
>
> *<u>The Most High is ruler</u> over the realm of mankind.* DANIEL 4:25

God's ultimate purposes cannot be thwarted, sabotaged, resisted, or overruled. If He has determined that something will be, it indeed will be.

> **God has displayed His infinite power to you your whole life. It has been evident every day and night as you observed His marvelous creation. It is God who gives you the breath to remain alive, the mind with which to conceive thoughts and set goals, and the strength to attempt to achieve those goals. He grants this even when you choose to act in ways that are directly opposed to Him. His choosing to let you engage in those rebellious acts, as well as be subjected to rebellious acts by others, is in keeping with His other traits of righteousness, justice, and love. God has the power to overcome any obstacle and resolve any difficulty you may face — nothing is impossible for Him.**

CHAPTER 12

God is Just and Righteous

Every thought God conceives, every verdict He pronounces, and every sentence He imposes is right.

Does the Creator of all things always do what is right? Can He be justly accused by any man of being unjust? He is all-knowing, all-wise, and all-powerful, and there is absolutely nothing beyond Him. Does He always employ these powers in ways that are fair and equitable? There is a simple answer.

God is just and righteous in all His dealings. Over and over again scripture affirms this.

> *All His ways are just; A God of faithfulness and without injustice, Righteous and upright is He.* DEUTERONOMY 32:4
>
> *Surely, God will not act wickedly, And the Almighty will not pervert justice.* JOB 34:12
>
> *For the Lord is righteous, He loves righteousness.* PSALM 11:7
>
> *He loves righteousness and justice.* PSALM 33:5

> *God is a righteous judge.* PSALM 7:11
>
> *For I, the Lord, love justice.* ISAIAH 61:8
>
> *Righteous and true are Your ways.* REVELATION 15:3

God is righteous and just in all His dealings because that is who He is at the core of His being. And this character trait has particular relevance to His verdicts and sentences.

A *verdict* is the finding or decision of a judge or jury in a criminal case, and typically involves a pronouncement of "guilty" or "not guilty" with respect to the charges in view. It is distinct from a *sentence,* which is the punishment or penalty imposed on the offender. Thus a judge may pass a verdict of guilty with respect to an individual charged with premeditated murder, and a sentence of life imprisonment or death.

In God's relationship with mankind, He likewise forms verdicts and passes sentences based on man's works. And in every single case, His verdicts and sentences are just and right.

God is impartial in His judgments. For God to be just, He must never show favoritism. This likewise has application not only to His verdicts, but also His sentences. While there is no shortage of judges in history who have made decisions based on their own biases, this is never the case with God.

> *God is the God of gods and the Lord of lords, the great, the mighty, and the awesome God who does not show partiality nor take a bribe. He executes justice.*
> DEUTERONOMY 10:16–18
>
> *The* LORD *our God will have no part in unrighteousness or partiality or the taking of a bribe.*
> 2 CHRONICLES 19:7

God is Just and Righteous

> *God is not one to show partiality.* ACTS 10:34

And of Himself God says:

> *I, the* LORD, *speak righteousness, Declaring things that are upright.* ISAIAH 45:19

Since God is just, it means every verdict He pronounces, and every sentence that flows out of that verdict, is absent of partiality. There is therefore no injustice in it at all.

God's verdicts are always accurate because they are rooted in His knowledge of all things. A human judge can pass a wrong verdict and unjustly condemn a man for various reasons: failure to have all the facts, testimony from false witnesses, and the like. But none of these things come into play with God. He has all facts in view from every conceivable perspective, and every motive is laid bare. His verdicts are therefore always perfect and without error.

God's sentences are never excessive. When a man is guilty of a certain offense, it is possible to impose a penalty which is too severe. But this is never the case with God. If He determines a certain offense warrants a particular punishment, then He not only has the power to effect that punishment, but that punishment is *right*. There is no injustice in it on account of its being too harsh, severe or disproportionate. The punishment is fitting, proper, and good.

God's sentences are never deficient. Just as it is possible to impose a penalty that is excessive, the same applies in the other direction — it is possible to impose a sentence that is too light. But this likewise is never the case with God. When the guilty stand before Him, His sentence is not too light. An inadequate sentence diminishes the gravity of the offense and constitutes an injustice. But God's sentences are good and right, imposing on the offender a punishment which perfectly matches the wrong committed.

God cannot conceive an unjust, unrighteous, evil thought. Every action God takes flows from thoughts within Himself that He alone has conceived. And the countless number of thoughts that He Himself knows are all good, just, holy and righteous. There is not even one *thought* that can be classified as evil, wrong, unjust or unrighteous; *not one*.

God Himself expressed how He cannot conceive evil thoughts when He addressed the exceedingly abominable and frequent practice of human sacrifice in ancient times. One particular false god was named Baal, and his temples and altars were often built at places of high elevation such as the tops of mountains or hills ("high places"). To those who were engaging in this brutal practice of human sacrifice, God said:

> *They have filled this place with the blood of the innocent and have built the high places of Baal to burn their sons in the fire as burnt offerings to Baal, a thing which I never commanded or spoke of, <u>nor did it ever enter My mind</u>.* JEREMIAH 19:5

The fact that God cannot conceive an unrighteous thought in no way diminishes His knowledge of all things. A man may not *conceive* an evil thought himself, but he may be very aware of the evil thoughts others have conceived. Even so God knows all things — even the evil thoughts of men — but He Himself never conceived such thoughts. He conceived and willed that man should be able to make choices, which is a good thing. But evil thoughts arising from men's hearts do not have their origin in God.

> **God is just and righteous at the core of His being. He is incapable of even conceiving within Himself an evil thought. Any action He takes is right, and any verdict or sentence He forms concerning you is just.**

Chapter 13

God Abounds in Truth

Any statement, assessment, or representation God makes concerning anything is true.

The world can view truth as relative — what is true for you is not true for me. Truth is not treated as something absolute. Besides such a view being self-contradicting, it is contrary to the revelation of God concerning Himself. God being truthful can be stated two ways: positively and negatively.

God perfectly declares what is and is not the case. Of Himself God says:

> *The* LORD, *the* LORD *God, compassionate and gracious, slow to anger, and abounding in lovingkindness <u>and truth</u>.* EXODUS 34:6

And scripture repeatedly affirms that God is truth.

> *You are near, O* LORD, *And <u>all Your commandments are truth</u>.* PSALM 119:151

Into Your hand I commit my spirit; You have ransomed me, O Lord, <u>*God of truth*</u>. Psalm 31:5

Now, O Lord God, *You are God, and <u>Your words are truth</u>.* 2 Samuel 7:28

Great and marvelous are Your works, O Lord God, the Almighty; Righteous and <u>true are Your ways</u>. Revelation 15:3

<u>*God is true*</u>. John 3:33

<u>*Him who is true*</u>. 1 John 5:20

<u>*He who sent Me is true*</u>. John 8:26

He who is blessed in the earth Will be blessed by the <u>God of truth</u>. Isaiah 65:16

If God says something is the case, then that is indeed the case. If He states such and such does not apply to a particular situation, then it truly does not apply. If anything God says is found to be untrue, it is not because what He said was untrue. It is because we misinterpreted what He said.

God cannot lie. He *cannot* say something that is untrue. This is basically saying the same things previously stated, but only negatively.

<u>*God … cannot lie*</u>. Titus 1:2

<u>*It is impossible for God to lie*</u>. Hebrews 6:18

<u>*God is not a man, that He should lie, Nor a son of man, that He should repent; Has He said, and will He not do it? Or has He spoken, and will He not make it good?*</u> Numbers 23:19

So we can say that any statement, assessment, or representation God makes concerning anything is perfectly true. But we can elaborate on this even more to make things more clear.

God never overstates or exaggerates the case. He does not make something bad sound worse than it is, nor does He make something good sound better than it is. If He says of mankind "There is none righteous, not even one" (ROMANS 3:10), then He means *not even one* person is righteous; it is not an overstatement. It is not as if *a few* are righteous, and God just exaggerated. Likewise if He says there is an afterlife where certain people will live in a new world and "there will no longer be any death; there will no longer be any mourning, or crying, or pain" (REVELATION 21:4), then it is not an exaggeration. Certain people will indeed experience a life after death which is *absolutely free* of mourning, crying, pain or death. It is not that there will be *some* pain and sorrow, and God just overstated things.

God's abounding in truth is rooted in His other perfections. If God did not possess His other traits, He either would not or could not be truthful. If He did not know everything, He may incorrectly assess something because He did not have all the facts. If He knew everything but was unrighteous, He might intentionally not tell the truth just to be spiteful. If He changed at the core of His being, then He might be truthful for one thousand years but then one day decide to take a hiatus from truth-telling.

Because God is eternal, always there, knows everything, created everything, and is righteous, it is *impossible* for Him to be mistaken about *anything*. Human limitations such as perceiving things incorrectly, showing favoritism, being prejudiced, or failing to word things correctly do not apply to Him.

> **God's words are true, and if He makes an assessment of the condition of your heart, it is accurate; if He makes a declaration regarding the quality of your works, it is correct; if He declares what your eternal destiny will be given certain conditions, it is a statement of fact.**

Chapter 14

God has Emotions and Feelings

God's emotions are as much a demonstration of His perfections as all His other qualities.

Thus far we have considered numerous aspects of God's nature and character — His being all knowing, all powerful, and other glorious traits. But within God these attributes are not void of an emotional dimension. Words such as "feelings" or "emotions" may be ascribed to God, provided such words are properly understood.

God can be pleased, grieved and provoked. Each of these emotions will be considered individually in future chapters. Here we are simply acknowledging these sensations do exist within God, but qualifying that fact with two very important points.

God's emotions are always righteous and good. He never has a feeling that fails to conform to what is just, proper and right.

Men are capable of experiencing emotions that are utterly contrary to what actually should be felt. The *type* of feeling is out of alignment with what should be. A sadistic man can find *pleasure* in harming others. A murderer can be *saddened* his evil plot was thwarted. And a robber can become *angry* he was caught in the act. These are all situations where the emotion experienced was an indication of corruption and depravity, for it is exactly opposite to what should be felt.

The corruption often present in man's emotions does not apply to God. If He has pleasure, it is because those feelings are in keeping with His holy, righteous, loving nature. If He is provoked to anger, it is likewise because it corresponds to His holy, righteous, loving nature. God never feels pleasure when there should grief, or a sense of indifference when there should be anger.

God's emotions are always proportionate. God's emotions are not only right because they do not evoke an opposite reaction, but because they evoke the correct reaction in proper measure.

Scripture contains many passages that show God's emotions exist in a spectrum. As respects God's anger, sometimes He is described as "angry," other times "very angry." And as respects pleasure, in the creation account each creative day we are told "God saw that it was good." But when all was completed we are told "God saw all that He had made, and behold, it was *very* good" (GENESIS 1:31).

In contrast to man, the varying degrees of emotion in God are but another aspect of His perfections. Human emotions or feelings can be disproportionate based on a variety of factors: tiredness, hunger, stress, and so on. What may cause one to be angry one day may cause him to be very angry another time; there is no consistency. But such mood swings do not apply to God.

> **The God who created you is capable of feeling pleasure, grief and anger. But He is never temperamental, and His emotions are never erratic. Whatever the situation or circumstance, His emotions are always right, proper and fitting both in type and degree.**

Chapter 15

God can be Pleased

God can experience delight, and He takes pleasure in many different things.

When we say God can be "pleased," we simply mean there is that which brings God pleasure and delight; a satisfaction, gratification, or gladness. What evokes these feelings are clearly detailed by God Himself and those who spoke of Him.

God takes pleasure in His loving, creative acts. The book of Genesis records God's creation of the universe. We read how He created light, the dry land and seas, vegetation, the stars, animals and insects, as well as man and woman. In each of these spectacular creative acts, over and over again the phrase is repeated "God saw that it was good" (GENESIS 1).

Just as a painter admires his painting, the architect his building, or the potter his pottery, even so God took satisfaction in creating the universe and all that is in it. When all the processes, life-forms, planets, stars, and sub-atomic particles were brought into being by the sheer power of His will, He beheld the beauty of the created order that sprung from those conceptions in His infinite mind. And His reaction to His creative work was simple yet profound.

> *God saw all that He had made, and behold, <u>it was very good</u>.* GENESIS 1:31

God's sense that His creation was "very good" was not simply in how precisely engineered and intricately designed everything was. It was also rooted in something much deeper to His loving heart: His delight in showing lovingkindness towards His creatures.

The original creation was beautiful, glorious and free of danger. Man was not subject to earthquakes, tornadoes, tsunamis, and other natural catastrophes. There also was no enmity between man and animals. Instead, the original creation was a safe, awe inspiring environment where man could live in peace and tranquility with nature, himself, and above all, with God. And it was this lovingkindness of God towards man in providing such an environment that God had delight.

A mother delights in providing loving care for her children, and a husband takes pleasure in providing a home for his beloved wife. Even so, God took great delight in placing man and woman in a world where they could experience joy, peace, tranquility, harmony, intimacy, and fellowship. It was indeed "very good."

God delights in lovingkindness, justice and righteousness. He says of Himself:

> *I am the* LORD *who exercises lovingkindness, justice and righteousness on earth; for <u>I delight in these things</u>.* JEREMIAH 9:24

In this verse, God is not speaking of His reaction to witnessing acts between a man and his fellow man. Instead He is describing what He Himself does, and how He Himself acts in relation to man. "*I* am the LORD *who exercises* lovingkindness, justice and righteousness on earth."

All God's dealings with man are demonstrations of His lovingkindness, justice and righteousness. This was true both in the original creation, and even after man's rebellion against God wherein the earth was cursed and chaos ensued.

God not only *is* just and righteous, He *delights* and takes *pleasure* in justice and righteousness.

> *For I, the Lord, love justice.* ISAIAH 61:8

God's love for justice means He delights in taking up the cause of the oppressed and the vulnerable. And He takes up their cause in two ways: by bringing judgment on their oppressors, and help to those in need. This is why over and over again God references widows, orphans, the poor, and the alien.

> *He executes justice for the orphan and the widow, and shows His love for the alien by giving him food and clothing.* DEUTERONOMY 10:18

> *The Lord performs righteous deeds And judgments for all who are oppressed.* PSALM 103:6

> *I know that the Lord will maintain the cause of the afflicted And justice for the poor.* PSALM 140:12

And it is because God delights in lovingkindness, justice and righteousness that He commands man to do the same.

> *Thus says the* LORD, *"Do justice and righteousness, and deliver the one who has been robbed from the power*

> *of his oppressor. Also do not mistreat or do violence to the stranger, the orphan, or the widow; and do not shed innocent blood in this place."* JEREMIAH 22:3

> *Thus has the* LORD *of hosts said, "Dispense true justice and practice kindness and compassion each to his brother; and do not oppress the widow or the orphan, the stranger or the poor; and do not devise evil in your hearts against one another."* ZECHARIAH 7:9–10

What pleases God can be defined both positively and negatively: by what He likes, and does not like; by what brings Him pleasure, and what does not bring Him pleasure. We have thus far considered only the positive aspects. But so as to leave no uncertainty in the matter, scripture provides specific details as to what brings God no pleasure.

God has no pleasure in the evil deeds of men. This is flipside of delighting in lovingkindness, justice and righteousness. When addressing those who had rebelled against His commands, He said:

> *I called, but no one answered; I spoke, but they did not listen. And they did evil in My sight And chose that in which I did not delight.* ISAIAH 66:4

God finds no delight when men engage in anything contrary to His moral will. When men worship false gods; when they, murder, lie, cheat, or blaspheme; when they act arrogantly, oppressively or with cruelty, God takes no pleasure in it. In fact He not only takes no pleasure in it, He *hates* it and is provoked by it.

God takes no pleasure in judging the wicked. When men persist in their evil deeds and God sentences them to death, He finds no joy in doing so.

> *"As I live!" declares the Lord* GOD, *"<u>I take no pleasure in the death of the wicked</u>, but rather that the wicked turn from his way and live."* EZEKIEL 33:11

> *"For <u>I have no pleasure in the death of anyone who dies</u>," declares the Lord* GOD. *"Therefore, repent and live."* EZEKIEL 18:32

A two-fold truth is presented here. First, God does not take pleasure even in the just execution of a wicked man. Yes, He delights in justice for it is disagreeable to let injustice remain. In the end He ensures justice prevails. But even in establishing justice God does not delight in death, but "rather that the wicked turn from his way and live." Second:

God takes pleasure in granting pardon and effecting restoration. When men repent and turn from their wicked ways, God delights in granting forgiveness and sparing their life.

> *Who is a God like You, who pardons iniquity ... <u>He delights in unchanging love</u>.* MICAH 7:18

Forgiveness, not judgment, is God's delight. Life, not death, is His pleasure. Kindness, not harshness, bring Him gladness.

> **God is about life, peace, tranquility, grace, mercy, kindness, caring, compassion, truth, justice, and forgiveness. He delights in these things. They were reflected in the original creation, and they are reflected even now in a fallen world where He seeks to grant forgiveness to you and avert your judgment.**

Chapter 16

God can be Grieved

Figuratively speaking, God can weep.

If God never created beings who were capable of defying Him, every act would always conform to His will. How can the sun or planets rebel against God? They have no such capacity. But in man God created beings who are free to resist and rebel against Him.

When man rebels, God grieves. And there is a three dimensional aspect to this grief. God grieves over the suffering others are subjected to when one rebels. He grieves over the judgment He may have to impose on the offender. And He grieves over all the blessings the sinner forfeited on account of his rebellion.

God grieves over the suffering and misery man's rebellion brings onto his fellow man. When a man steals, the owner experiences loss. When a vengeful man injures another, he brings pain and suffering on the victim. When men oppress, they cause heartache and exasperation to those whom they afflict. And even when men sin and there appears to be no negative consequence to another human being, even then the

God can be Grieved

man has ultimately harmed himself. These are all cases where suffering is directly caused by human agency through acts which God did not morally approve. In all such situations, God grieves.

Suffering is definitely part of the human experience, but the fact is most suffering is directly related to the nature of the offense in relation to God's created order. If a parent commands a child not to touch the fire, and the child rebels and reaches for the flame, that child will be burned. Even so, rebellion against God has immediate negative, harmful consequences to the individual and to others.

The story of Noah is a clear example of God's capacity to grieve. We are told:

> *Then the* LORD *saw that the wickedness of man was great on the earth, and that every intent of the thoughts of his heart was only evil continually. The <u>Lord was sorry</u> that He had made man on the earth, and <u>He was grieved</u> in His heart.* GENESIS 6:5–6

> *The* LORD *said, "… <u>I am sorry</u> that I have made them."* GENESIS 6:7

> *The earth was corrupt in the sight of God, and the earth was filled with violence.* GENESIS 6:11

It is important to process this description of man's corruption in light of God's attributes. In this passage the corruption primarily consisted of violence for "the earth was *filled* with *violence*." There were assaults, fights, rapes, robberies, murders and the like. God, who is always there, witnessed every single one of those violent acts first hand. Furthermore God, who knows all things, saw this outward violence flowed from a heart that was utterly corrupt. These acts were born of an illicit desire for power, money, prestige, vengeance, or sexual gratification. In other cases the violence was committed simply for sport and born of a depraved sense of amusement and diversion. Whatever the case, *every* intent of the thoughts of man's heart; *everything* he desired and contemplated doing; *every* thought he conceived was only evil *continually*.

Man's corruption is clearly laid out in these verses, but so is God's reaction. He was "grieved in His heart" and "sorry" He had made man. God's sorrow was not an indication He was unaware things would turn out that way, and it was not as if He viewed His decision to make man a mistake. God *never* makes a mistake; *never*. Rather God being "sorry" was simply another way of expressing God's grieving over the miserable state of affairs man had placed himself.

Another account of God's grieving over man's rebellion is that of ancient Israel in the desert. It is written:

> *How often they rebelled against Him in the wilderness*
> *And grieved Him in the desert! Again and again they*
> *tempted God, And pained the Holy One of Israel.*
> PSALM 78:40–41

Examining the history of Israel to which this passage refers, one can read how the Israelites engaged in numerous evil acts: idolatry, sexual immorality, murmuring, blasphemy, hatred, covetousness, thanklessness, and the like. How was God affected by all this? He was "grieved" and "pained" by it.

These two accounts are considering God's grieving only from the perspective of the destructive, built-in, negative consequences in relation to one's fellow man. But in both these accounts God was also grieved other ways.

God grieves over the judgment He is obligated to impose on unrepentant sinners. God says:

> *"As I live!" declares the Lord* GOD, *"I take no pleasure in the death of the wicked, but rather that the wicked turn from his way and live."* EZEKIEL 33:11

> *"For I have no pleasure in the death of anyone who dies," declares the Lord* GOD. *"Therefore, repent and live."* EZEKIEL 18:32

God is just and righteous, and He will not let injustice go unpunished forever. Justice will be served. In the days of Noah God ultimately brought a flood to execute evildoers for their sins. And with Israel in the desert numerous judgments were imposed that took their lives. But in both cases, God grieved. He took no pleasure in imposing His righteous judgments.

God grieves over the blessings man forfeits through his rebellion. In one place God expresses His heart's desire saying:

> *Oh that they had such a heart in them, that they would fear Me and keep all My commandments always, that it may be well with them and with their sons forever!* DEUTERONOMY 5:29

This verse reveals the heart cry of God towards man in general. God does not desire harm, hurt, disease, suffering, heartache and death. He desires things to "be well" with people. He desires life, goodness, fullness and wellbeing. But man's refusal to live as God intends, his insistence on doing things his own way, and his obstinance in rejecting all appeals to turn around result not only in suffering in the present, but loss of potential blessings in the future.

How many parents drowned in the days of Noah who could have had their family lines remain if only those parents had repented? How many Israelites perished in the desert who likewise could have had joyful, fulfilling lives had they only turned? But they missed out on all God had for them. On account of that unrealized future, God grieved.

> **When you rebel against God, He grieves over that suffering and loss you inflicted on yourself and others that was inherent in the offense. He grieves if He has to judge you for that rebellion, and also over all the blessing you forfeited.**

Chapter 17

God can be Provoked

God's anger is roused on account of man's rebellion, but it is always just and appropriate.

The realization that an all-knowing, all-wise, all-powerful God can get angry is truly a frightful and terrifying thing. After all He is always there, and can do anything, at anytime, in anyway He pleases. But God becoming angry must be viewed in light of His other attributes, and what scripture teaches about His anger.

God's anger is always right. If it were not so, He could not be righteous. But *everything* God feels or does is *always* right — it is impossible for it to be otherwise. So if God is angry, it is an expression of His righteous, loving character just as much as all His other attributes.

Anger is often viewed as a negative, unrighteous emotion, and this is understandable in light of man's anger. Men not only get angry for illegitimate reasons, but even when they are angry for the right reason they can channel their anger in ways that are disproportionate to the offense. A person who is called a derogatory name can physically assault the name-caller. Man's anger is therefore often unrighteous and a reflection of his fallen nature.

God does not share in the weaknesses of man. He does not act rashly and out of proportion with the offense. He only becomes angry when there is just cause to be so.

God's righteous anger is rooted in His love of justice and truth, and His hatred for injustice and evil. When God is angry it is because something has gone seriously askew in the created order, and that something is that which He hates. And that which He hates are the evil works of men who engage in practices He despises and abhors.

> *There are six things which <u>the Lord hates</u>, Yes, seven which are <u>an abomination</u> to Him: Haughty eyes, a lying tongue, And hands that shed innocent blood, A heart that devises wicked plans, Feet that run rapidly to evil, A false witness who utters lies, And one who spreads strife among brothers.* PROVERBS 6:16–19

> *"Let none of you devise evil in your heart against another, and do not love perjury; for all these are <u>what I hate</u>,"* declares the LORD. ZECHARIAH 8:17

The scriptures above are by no means exhaustive of what God hates. Nor should it be thought that unless God specifically says He hates something, He therefore either approves of or is indifferent towards it. God's hatred of evil works is evident from various accounts in scripture where He was "provoked to anger."

Over the course of Israel's history, God was repeatedly provoked to anger by Israel's worship of false gods. This worship involved various abominable practices, human sacrifice often being one of them. Given God's loving, just, caring nature, He was infuriated over these depraved practices.

> *<u>With abominations they provoked Him to anger.</u> They sacrificed to demons who were not God, To gods whom they have not known, New gods who came lately.*
> DEUTERONOMY 32:16–17

> *The sons of Israel did evil in the sight of the LORD and served the Baals, and they forsook the LORD ... and followed other gods from among the gods of the peoples who were around them, and bowed themselves down to them; thus they provoked the LORD to anger. So they forsook the LORD and served Baal and the Ashtaroth. The <u>anger of the Lord burned</u> against Israel.* JUDGES 2:11–14

> *The LORD said to the sons of Israel, "Did I not deliver you from the Egyptians, the Amorites, the sons of Ammon, and the Philistines? Also when the Sidonians, the Amalekites and the Maonites oppressed you, you cried out to Me, and I delivered you from their hands. Yet you have forsaken Me and served other gods; therefore <u>I will no longer deliver you. Go and cry out to the gods which you have chosen; let them deliver you in the time of your distress.</u>"* JUDGES 10:11–14

These passages are just a small portion of a recurring theme in scripture: man's rebellion and evil arouse God's anger. And He has a strong aversion to evil deeds because they bring into His creation that which is contrary to His very nature. God's character is life, blessing, fullness, righteousness and truth. But man's rebellion brings evil, suffering, heartache, injustice and death. God therefore becomes indignant and is minded to enforce justice to rectify the situation.

God is slow to anger. Of Himself God says:

> *The* Lord, *the* Lord *God, compassionate and gracious, slow to anger, and abounding in lovingkindness and truth.* Exodus 34:6

God being slow to anger means He is patient and forbearing. He does not immediately judge those who rebel, even though He is within His rights to do so. He gives opportunity for sinners to repent so they can avert judgment, and He sends His messengers to warn of that judgment.

> *The Lord has sent to you all His servants the prophets again and again, but you have not listened nor inclined your ear to hear, saying, "Turn now everyone from his evil way and from the evil of your deeds … and do not go after other gods to serve them and to worship them, and do not provoke Me to anger with the work of your hands, and I will do you no harm." Yet you have not listened to Me, declares the* Lord, *in order that you might provoke Me to anger with the work of your hands to your own harm.* Jeremiah 25:4–7

God sending His servants to warn is born of His taking no pleasure in the death of the wicked. God desires to grant life, and He would rather the wicked turn and be spared. In His forbearance, He patiently and repeatedly warns those over whom judgment is hovering.

God being slow to anger means He is not quick-tempered. When considering human behavior, being slow to anger is cited as a virtue and contrasted with those who are easily angered. "He who is slow to anger has great understanding, But he who is quick-tempered exalts folly" (PROVERBS 14:29). "A hot-tempered man stirs up strife, But the slow to anger calms a dispute" (PROVERBS 15:18). Even so, God is not one to react irrationally or impetuously in outbursts of wrath. His anger is aroused in the context of His having patiently endured being continually offended; of His having exercised great restraint against those to whom judgment is due.

God's righteous anger, if not appeased, ultimately culminates in judgment. He determines what is the just and fair punishment for those who defy Him. And He, in accordance with His infinite power over all creation, ensures that penalty is put into effect. And He can impose that penalty in a variety of ways.

> *Then the Lord rained on Sodom and Gomorrah brimstone and fire from the* LORD *out of heaven, and He overthrew those cities, and all the valley, and all the inhabitants of the cities, and what grew on the ground.* GENESIS 19:24-25

> *And the Lord rained hail on the land of Egypt … The hail struck all that was in the field through all the land of Egypt, both man and beast; the hail also struck every plant of the field and shattered every tree of the field.* EXODUS 9:23–25

> *The Lord hurled a great wind on the sea and there was a great storm on the sea so that the ship was about to break up.* JONAH 1:4

> *The Lord sent fiery serpents* among the people and they bit the people, so that many people of Israel died. **NUMBERS 21:6**
>
> *So the Lord sent a pestilence* on Israel; 70,000 men of Israel fell. **1 CHRONICLES 21:14**
>
> *The Lord sent lions* among them which killed some of them. **2 KINGS 17:25**

This is just a small portion of the many scriptures detailing God's wrath against those who rebelled against Him. God employed other means to bring judgment such as earthquakes, flooding, insect infestations, barrenness, and invasions by hostile armies. God rules heaven and earth, so He is able to use all these, and any other means He chooses, to effect His righteous judgment.

We must be careful not to err on either side of what scripture teaches about God's anger. It is a very serious error to think every natural catastrophe, animal attack, illness, war, or other tragedy is God punishing people. This is utterly false. But it is also untrue to say God never employs these things as punishment. God does become angry over man's rebellion, and He has used these things in the past, and will continue to use them in the future as He deems appropriate.

In this fallen world there will always be people in authority who act corruptly. Whether it be dictators who rule countries, employers who manage employees, or parents who manage households, there will be those who oppress, abuse and take advantage of those over whom they have oversight. We fear making those who rule us angry, knowing what those leaders or managers can do. After all, they may have the authority to unjustly deny a valuable privilege, unfairly release us from employment, blackmail us, impose a harsh fine, imprison us without cause, or even sentence us to death.

Should the fear of provoking a corrupt leader compare with the fear of provoking the righteous, almighty Creator of the universe? To make corrupt human leaders angry is one thing; their anger is a display of their own unjust judgment and depravity. But to make a righteous *God* angry is to arouse the wrath of Him who patiently endured our rebellion and is poised to judge with absolute power.

> *It is a terrifying thing to fall into the hands of the living God.* HEBREWS 10:31

Indeed, how fearful it is to be subject to the wrath of God.

> **God can become angry on your account. His anger is always righteous and in keeping with His love for justice and truth. He does not immediately judge you on account of your rebellion, but desires to grant mercy and forgiveness. This is ultimately the message in John 3:16.**

Chapter 18

God is Love

God is compassionate, gracious, slow to anger and abounding in lovingkindness.

The New Testament makes a profound statement.

<u>God is love</u>. 1 John 4:8

Love may be considered by way of definition, and also by examples of its demonstration. The quintessential example of God's love is the message in John 3:16:

> *For God so loved the world, that He gave His only begotten Son, that whoever believes in Him shall not perish, but have eternal life.* John 3:16

How this message demonstrates God's love will be fully revealed as this Good News in John 3:16 book series unfolds, so we will not expand on this quintessential demonstration here. However there are many other ways in scripture and in life that God shows His love, and we will consider these later on in this chapter.

As respects definition, how "God is love" is clearly defined in a revelation God gave of Himself early on in the Bible. In keeping with His perfect knowledge, He details five of His own character traits.

> *The* LORD, *the* LORD *God, <u>compassionate and gracious,
> slow to anger</u>, and abounding in <u>lovingkindness</u> and
> <u>truth.</u>* EXODUS 34:6

The first four of these five traits can be considered different aspects of love. In other words, to say "God is love" is the same as saying "God is compassionate, gracious, slow to anger, and abounding in lovingkindness." This verse is frequently referenced in Old Testament history, and it perfectly encapsulates what is meant in the New Testament phrase "God is love."

These four traits of God's love are all related and overlap. A loving act of God may equally be considered an instance of His being compassionate, gracious, slow to anger and abounding in lovingkindness. It is best not to be too strict in considering Old Testament examples, as if we can form some sort of classification and say "Here are examples of compassion," "Here are examples graciousness," and so on. On the contrary, any of the examples we consider lend themselves to one as well as the other.

God is compassionate. He empathizes with the suffering of the afflicted and heartbroken, and is moved to take steps to deliver them from their plight.

The story of God's deliverance of Israel from slavery through Moses is a classic example of God's compassion. In the midst of their brutal oppression God said:

> <u>I have surely seen the affliction</u> of My people who are
> in Egypt, <u>and have given heed to their cry</u> because of
> their taskmasters, for <u>I am aware of their sufferings</u>.

> *So I have come down to deliver them from the power of the Egyptians.* EXODUS 3:7–8

In these verses God repeatedly references His understanding of the misery of the Israelites, and His simultaneous determination to end their suffering. God said He had not just "seen" but He had "surely seen" their affliction. He had "given heed" to their cry, was "aware of their suffering," and had "come down to deliver them." All these phrases reveal God not as a casual observer of the Israelites, viewing their plight in a clinical, dispassionate, analytical way. He pitied their condition and suffered with them, being fully aware of their fears, abuse and oppression. And it was in the context of that understanding that He determined to free them from bondage.

God is gracious. He is merciful and forgiving, granting pardon to the unjust and favor to the undeserving. This grace works in conjunction with His compassion. He is sympathetic of the plight sinners have placed themselves in by being liable to God's judgment, and He desires their deliverance from the judgment He Himself is obligated in justice to impose.

God forgiving those who were completely undeserving of any such favor occurs numerous times throughout Old Testament history. Over and over again individuals, people groups or nations are not only pardoned for their wrongdoing, but shown favor above and beyond that which they should have received in light of their works.

- David committed adultery with Bathsheba, and then had her husband killed so as to take her as wife and cover it up. But God spared David the death penalty and granted Solomon be born through her. 2 SAMUEL 11:1-12:24.

- Ten times the Israelites murmured against God even though He had miraculously delivered them from bondage in Egypt, and He set His mind to destroy them. But through the intercession of Moses He spared the entire nation the death penalty and led them in the wilderness for forty years with a cloud by day, a pillar of fire by night, and manna from heaven. NUMBERS 14.

- The Israelites became ensnared with worshiping false gods in the land of Canaan, and for this God delivered them into slavery through other nations. But in the midst of their oppression when they cried out to the Lord, He raised up a deliverer who delivered them from bondage and under whom Israel prospered. JUDGES 2.

- Through the prophet Jonah God warned the exceedingly cruel people of Ninevah of their impending judgment. But when they repented, God relented and spared everyone. JONAH 1-4

This quality in God to kindly pardon can be put this way:

> *He has not dealt with us according to our sins, Nor rewarded us according to our iniquities.* PSALM 103:10

It is God's nature and disposition to forgive, not judge; to show mercy, not coldheartedness.

God is slow to anger. We have previously considered this trait in noting God can be provoked, but it bears repeating. God is patient and shows great restraint when witnessing the injustices man commits against his fellow man and against God Himself. Instead of immediately becoming angry and judging those who rightly deserve punishment, He patiently endures.

God's being slow to anger is rooted in His displeasure in judging sinners. This is something God Himself declares, and He even prefaced the statement with a solemn oath ("as I live") to reinforce the truthfulness of it.

> *Say to them, "As I live!" declares the Lord* GOD, *"I take no pleasure in the death of the wicked, but rather that the wicked turn from his way and live. <u>Turn back, turn back from your evil ways! Why then will you die,</u> O house of Israel?"* EZEKIEL 33:11

In the history of Israel and even foreign nations, God exercised great forbearance. Though abominations were committed time and time again, it was years before judgment would finally fall. And it came only after those nations failed to heed the warnings of impending doom God made through His prophets.

God abounds in lovingkindness. It is expressed in His tender care and goodness towards His creation. God is a God of goodwill; a God who desires to impart joy, satisfaction, and fulfillment. His desire has always been for man's wellbeing, and His lovingkindness "abounds" both in the depth and frequency of its display. There are numerous examples in the Old Testament.

- helping Abraham find his son a suitable bride through his servant. GENESIS 24:12-16

- giving Joseph who had been unjustly imprisoned favor before the chief jailer. GENESIS 39:21-23

- granting pardon to the Israelites and sparing them death by pestilence through Moses' petition. NUMBERS 11:17-20

- providing the Israelites food and water during their wanderings in the wilderness. PSALM 107:1-9

It is not an overstatement to say there are literally thousands of examples where God shows His lovingkindness. The sun providing light so we can see; the streams and springs providing water so we may drink; or the plants and animals providing food so we may eat. The companionship of a friend; the kiss of a spouse; or the closeness of a family gathering. An occupation so we can earn a living, or a home so we can have shelter. These can all be deemed examples of God's lovingkindness — displays of His tender and benevolent concern and affection.

> **God loves you. He understands your suffering and is moved by your plight. He seeks to deliver you and bring you into a life of fullness, goodness, and well-being. Though you have rebelled against Him, He is slow to anger. His desire is for you to be forgiven. Every day in hundreds of ways that you are not even aware, He displays His lovingkindness towards you.**

CHAPTER 19

"God" as used in John 3:16

For God so loved the world, that He gave His only begotten Son, that whoever believes in Him shall not perish, but have eternal life. JOHN 3:16

We are now in a position to expand on the word "God" as used in the powerful message of John 3:16. At the outset of this book we noted every word in this verse has a deep, clear meaning, and there is a specific way Jesus would have us understand "God," "gave," "Son," "believes," "perish," and "eternal life." These words reflect six core teachings of Jesus' worldview, and provide insight into understanding God, life and the hereafter. We can now consider just one of those six core teachings: the nature and character of "God."

We have used the Bible as the basis of our understanding who God is. The Old Testament contains the same scriptures Jesus Himself deemed authoritative. There are without question countless conceptions of God throughout history and even today. But to project onto the word "God" in John 3:16 any of those false conceptions is to distort the entire message. Our understanding of "God" must conform to the revelation God provided through His prophets, Christ Himself and His apostles. If we take into account the many scriptures that have been cited throughout this book, John 3:16 would read as follows.

> *There is only one God, and it is He who created all things. He is incorporeal, has no form and is always there. He is eternal, having no beginning and no end. He is all-knowing, all-wise and all-powerful. He is just, righteous and abounds in truth. He can be pleased, grieved and provoked. He is love; He is compassionate, gracious, slow to anger, and abounding in lovingkindness. This God so loved the world, that He gave His only begotten Son, that whoever believes in Him shall not perish, but have eternal life.* JOHN 3:16

May God grant that we begin to understand all the glorious, awe-inspiring truths encompassed in the word "God." For if we even had a faint understanding, we would fall on our face in worship to *Him who has no beginning and no end.*

THE NATURE AND CHARACTER OF GOD

Suggested Reading

This book was first published in 2020 — some forty years after I converted to Christianity. Over those years I have been exposed to many excellent teachings from pastors, Bible teachers, and godly men. Hearing a sermon, reading a Christian book, consulting a commentary, or just spending time in casual discussion have all no doubt played a role in my understanding of God. I am thankful to the Lord for all these experiences. But I can also say — God is witness — the vast majority of my understanding has been born of being like a Berean who "examined the Scriptures daily to see whether these things were so" (Acts 17:11).

In keeping with my own practice, but more-so with a view for the reader to "accurately handle the word of truth" (2 Timothy 2:15), by far the foremost book I can suggest reading is the Bible itself. Read it, patiently compare scripture with scripture, and prayerfully contemplate its meaning. "The Lord will give you understanding in everything" (2 Timothy 2:7). At the same time, since God has appointed pastors and teachers for edification, and also in recognition of human frailty, consult multiple works. To that end below is an alphabetical listing of reference tools and reading materials.

Blayney, B., Thomas Scott, and R.A. Torrey with Canne, John, Browne. *The Treasury of Scripture Knowledge*. London: Samuel Bagster and Sons, n.d.

Erickson, Millard J. *Christian Theology*. 3rd ed. Grand Rapids, MI: Baker Academic, 2013.

Grudem, Wayne A. *Systematic Theology: An Introduction to Biblical Doctrine*. Leicester, England; Grand Rapids, MI: Inter-Varsity Press; Zondervan Pub. House, 2004.

Faithlife LLC, *Logos Bible Software*. Bellingham, WA

Manser, Martin H. *Dictionary of Bible Themes: The Accessible and Comprehensive Tool for Topical Studies*. London: Martin Manser, 2009.

Spence-Jones, H. D. M., ed. *The Pulpit Commentary*. London; New York: Funk & Wagnalls Company, 1909.

Visit Rushwave.org

*Establishing Believers
in the Christian Faith*

*This book is available as a paperback,
hardcover, e-book, audiobook, and video*